Pets at Risk

From Allergies to Cancer,
Remedies for an Unsuspected Epidemic

ALFRED J. PLECHNER, D.V.M.
WITH MARTIN ZUCKER

Foreword by
Albert J. Simpson, D.V.M.

NEWSAGE I
TROUTDALE, (

PETS AT RISK:
From Allergies to Cancer,
Remedies for an Unsuspected Epidemic
Copyright © 2003 Alfred J. Plechner and Martin Zucker
ISBN 0-939165-48-1

NewSage Press
PO Box 607
Troutdale, OR 97060-0607
503-695-2211

website: www.newsagepress.com
email: info@newsagepress.com

Cover and Book Design by Sherry Wachter
Printed in the United States on recycled paper with soy ink.
Distributed in the United States and Canada by Publishers Group West

Note to the Reader: This book is not intended as medical advice or to replace veterinary care. It is meant exclusively for informational and educational purposes. If your animal has signs of illness, consult a qualified veterinarian. If your animal is currently taking medication, do not discontinue or substitute them for any suggestions described in this book without consulting your veterinarian.

LIBRARY OF CONGRESS CATALOGING-IN-PUBLICATION DATA

Plechner, Alfred J.
Pets at risk : from allergies to cancer, remedies for an unsuspected
epidemic / by Alfred J. Plechner with Martin Zucker ; foreword by Albert
J. Simpson.
    p. cm.
Includes bibliographical references (p.   ).
ISBN 0-939165-48-1
1. Dogs—Diseases—Treatment. 2. Cats—Diseases—Treatment.
3.Veterinary epidemiology. I. Zucker, Martin. II. Title.
SF991.P56 2003
636.7'0896--dc21
                                                                                2003014190

1 2 3 4 5 6 7 8 9

Dedication

*To the many people whose trust
enabled me to make a difference
in the lives of their animal companions.*

Table of Contents

TABLE OF CONTENTS

FOREWORD

Soon after starting out in veterinary practice I became aware that I was seeing a repetitive parade of ten or fifteen animals a day with the same problems for which I was using the same standard medications. I was not curing anything—just temporarily masking over the clinical signs of illness that I saw. I felt like a trained monkey doing the same tricks over and over.

Out of frustration I quit veterinary practice, changed careers, and joined a large corporation. But I deeply missed working with pets, and seven years later I decided to return to veterinary practice and give it another chance. My hope was that I might find new inspiration and treatments with which to really help animals.

About six months or so into my resurrected veterinary career, a new client brought a little red book into the office and showed it to me. It was *Pet Allergies: Remedies for an Epidemic,* by Alfred J. Plechner, D.V.M.

"This book is all about my dog," the client said. "Nobody has been able to do anything for my dog. Could you read this information and see if there is anything here that can help?"

Initially I scoffed at the thought of a client challenging me. But I agreed to read the book. To my surprise, I was amazed by what I read. I had never learned anything like this in veterinary school or read about it in a veterinary journal. Nobody had ever taught me to connect defective adrenal glands to estrogen, thyroid, and a malfunctioning immune system. The information made sense and I decided to follow up on it. I called Al Plechner. He answered all my questions and invited me to visit his clinic in Los Angeles to see firsthand what he was doing.

I took him up on the offer. Either he had made a major discovery or this was totally bogus. I would see for myself. I flew to Los Angeles and spent a full day with him. He assigned one of his assistants to me, opened his files for me to review, and invited me into the exam rooms to observe the treatments and talk to his clients.

I was impressed by Plechner's sincerity and the feedback I heard from the pet owners. This indeed appeared to be a major discovery. I felt that somebody had given me the missing pieces to a jigsaw puzzle I had been trying to solve for years.

Back home, I quickly put Plechner's principles to the test. I chose hopeless animals whose owners had spent hundreds of dollars trying to save. Now the animals were likely going to be put down. I asked the owners if they would allow me to try something new—a little known procedure I had learned from another veterinarian.

Most said yes and those who did got a great surprise. The results were extraordinary. The procedure worked in each and every case.

The first case I treated was an old Labrador named Clark. The dog had thickened skin, bacterial and yeast infections, and intermittent bloody diarrhea. His owners had brought him in to be euthanized. On Plechner's program, Clark made a remarkable recovery within six weeks, and lived in relatively good health for another two years before dying from a heart condition he had all his life.

As I began having dramatic successes with other animals my staff became transformed. Usually they were depressed whenever a hopeless case came in for euthanasia. At first, they were surprised by the results they witnessed. Then they actually started encouraging pet owners who called about euthanasia arrangements. "We may really be able to turn your animal around," they would tell them.

This book you are about to read is a major expansion of that little red book I first read some years ago. It goes far beyond allergies and reveals how a widespread but unrecognized glitch in the hormonal output of an animal can cause many of the serious diseases that bring down our pets.

This book is an eye-opener. For veterinarians, it fills a big knowledge gap and opens a broad avenue into effective prevention and healing. For pet owners, the book is a blueprint for forging a dynamic partnership with veterinarians that can preserve the health of vulnerable animals and restore the health of those who are sick. This information is decades ahead of mainstream veterinary medicine.

—Albert J. Simpson, D.V.M.,
Oregon City, Oregon

PREFACE

Americans pay a staggering $12 billion a year to veterinarians. Yet huge numbers of pets still die or become sick before their time. I believe much of this has to do with unsuspected hormonal imbalances that destabilize and weaken the immune system of animals, degrade their natural protection against illness, and rob them of health and longevity.

Other veterinarians refer many "end-of-the-line animals" to me. The owners bring in their sick pets and tell me that veterinarian So-and-So says, "The only thing really left to do is put the animal to sleep." In some very advanced cases that may be true, but in a vast majority of situations there is hope and there is a solution. This is why I have written this book.

Hormonal and immune interactions involve a vast and complex interaction of biochemicals that govern and protect the body. Medical science does not yet clearly understand these countless interactions. Many years ago as a young practitioner I tried to figure out why so many of my patients were getting sick and not responding to standard treatments. My clinical detective work led me along a path of discovery to a major hormonal-immune system disturbance that starts in the adrenal glands and causes a ripple effect of disorders ranging from common skin allergies to catastrophic autoimmune disease and cancer. I learned how to identify and correct this problem and create a successful program that to date has helped more than 50,000 of my own patients as well as many animals treated at other veterinary clinics.

Devastating endocrine-immune imbalances result from an unsuspected deficiency or defect in cortisol, an important adrenal hormonal. I correct this deficiency by using very low dosages of cortisone on a long-term basis. Cortisone is the pharmaceutical equivalent of the body's own cortisol. In my practice I use both synthetic cortisone medications and a natural cortisol preparation, and when used at very low dosages they represent safe and significant healing agents for many seemingly unrelated diseases.

In human medicine, the long-term, low-dosage cortisone approach has been pioneered by William Jefferies, M.D., an emeritus clinical professor of internal medicine at the University of Virginia. Now in his eighties, Jefferies has reported for years how this method can safely and effectively improve the condition of patients with allergies, chronic fatigue, and autoimmune disorders. Yet, just as in veterinary medicine, this effective treatment for humans has been generally ignored or overlooked.

Until recently, Jefferies and I were not aware of our parallel work—one in human medicine, the other in veterinary medicine. We met for the first time in 2002 when I was invited to present my findings to physicians at a conference sponsored by the Broda O. Barnes M.D. Research Foundation in Trumbull, Connecticut.

Cortisone has a big stigma attached to it. But, as both Jefferies and I found independently, the problem of side effects relates largely to the use of powerful, pharmacologic dosages, and not to smaller, physiologic dosages. This is an important distinction. So, too, is the understanding of small, physiologic dosages of natural cortisol or synthetic cortisone medications used as a form of hormone replacement to compensate for a hormone defect.

This book is about these distinctions and how they lead to great healing where other approaches fail.

I have shared my knowledge of this program with interested veterinarians internationally. Using this information, they, too, have been able to restore many hopeless cases. But I want many more veterinarians and pet owners to have this knowledge and apply it to restore the health of sick animals as well as to prevent ill health in the first place.

The strategies in my program include a blood test that veterinarians can use to precisely determine the presence of hormonal-immune malfunction. This book instructs veterinarians on how to obtain the blood test through veterinary laboratories and then translate the results into an individually effective hormone replacement program.

But recovery is not just dependent on the veterinarian doing all the work. Equally crucial is the pet owner's understanding, support, and active involvement in the process. In other words, this is a partnership between pet owner and veterinarian. There are things that only a veterinarian can do, and there are things that only a pet owner can do.

The first section of the book introduces the hormonal disturbance and its destructive effect on the immune system and health. I explain the sequence of events in an easy-to-understand way, so the reader develops a good grasp on what may be causing the animal's health problems. I also explain how the pet's diet can have a critical effect—

negative or positive—on condition and recovery. The information includes my "HIT list"—High In Trouble—foods that I find to be the most frequent cause of allergic reactions.

Part Two of *Pets at Risk* contains the precise steps on how to identify and correct the hormonal disturbance. Details on blood tests, interpretation of the tests, and administration of appropriate therapy are intended primarily to guide veterinarians but I invite pet owners to read the material and learn how the therapeutic process works. This information is not found in veterinary textbooks; however, it is based on the experience I have gained from thousands of successful cases and reports I have published in veterinary and medical journals.

Once the veterinarian interprets the test results and places the pet on corrective therapy, the pet owner will need to take an active role in the process. That means feeding a simple, nonallergenic diet to help support the recovery and good health of the pet. This is an extremely important aspect of the program, and not to be taken lightly, because the wrong food can totally thwart the therapeutic program.

If followed carefully, the program in this book can turn around even very sick animals, and do so rapidly. It is also an approach that I believe may offer significant insights for the treatment of human illnesses.

—Alfred J. Plechner, D.V.M.
LOS ANGELES, CALIFORNIA

As a health writer, I have the privilege to interview doctors in both human and veterinary medicine who I consider to be "true healers." These are dedicated and innovative individuals who explore outside the boundaries of formal medical training and conventional practices to seek better ways to help their patients. They are not satisfied with just giving temporary relief of symptoms. They try to prevent illness from occurring in the first place. Al Plechner is one such doctor.

"I'm just a plain-wrapped veterinarian," Al insists. He may be plain wrapped, but he is a sharp clinician and compassionate healer. More than three decades ago, he began searching for answers to frustrating clinical cases that his veterinary school training did not provide. He found answers by creating hypoallergenic diets for pets. His lamb and rice formulation for food-sensitive pets was so good it became a widely copied national bestseller.

Without any outside funding, he conducted his own clinical investigations and made the stunning discovery of a hormonal defect that incapacitates the immune system of pets. He learned how to correct the defect, and in the process, restore health to chronically sick patients, save acutely ill patients, and prevent disease in many susceptible animals.

Medicine, and indeed all science, advances because of the determination, vision, inventiveness, and courage of individuals. It is irrelevant to me whether those individuals are well-funded researchers or solo practitioners—hands-on, plain-wrapped people like Al Plechner—who make discoveries and find that their patients respond.

In the 1980s, Al and I collaborated to write a book on his approach to pet allergies. The response was very positive. Many veterinarians who read *Pet Allergies: Remedies for an Epidemic* tried Al's method and have used it with success in their practices. This new book goes far beyond allergies and addresses an epidemic of chronic disease among pets. It provides a comprehensive program with clear-cut directions sharpened by time and practice that has the potential to rescue many animals from a lifetime of suffering.

My hope is that this book reaches pet owners and breeders looking for answers to their animals' health problems that have not responded to current-day treatments. I hope also the book reaches open-minded veterinarians who are similarly looking for answers. Years ago, Al Plechner searched long and hard and found the answers he was looking for to rescue dogs and cats at high risk. If you are looking for answers, this book has a lot of them.

—Martin Zucker
LOS ANGELES, CALIFORNIA

Part One
THE EPIDEMIC

– ONE –

Endangered Dogs and Cats

Veterinarians are frustrated. They treat pets engulfed by relentless disorders with multiple and seemingly unrelated clinical signs. Frequently they can do little more than temporarily relieve their patients and make them more comfortable, but are unsuccessful in reversing the decline in vitality and health, or the course of disease. Many times they have no choice but to euthanize hopelessly sick pets, even young ones. On a daily basis veterinarians see animals such as the following cases I have worked with:

- Georgette, a beautiful three-year-old Golden Retriever, developed the canine equivalent of breast cancer. Another veterinarian had removed the mammary gland tumor and treated the dog with radiation. Within weeks, however, an adjacent mammary gland became cancerous. The vet removed the new tumor and again treated the dog with radiation. At this point, the veterinarian was extremely pessimistic about the chances for survival and indicated to the owners that the dog probably had no more than three to six months to live.
- Miles, a seven-year-old Airedale weighing just over a hundred pounds, had developed aggressive behavior and bitten one of his owners on two occasions. Just prior to these attacks, a strange expression of rage suddenly appeared on Miles's face. Something had to be done or else Miles would probably have to be euthanized.
- Buster was dying. This six-year-old domestic longhair cat had been previously diagnosed with feline leukemia and treated with chemotherapy by another veterinarian. By the time I treated Buster, he had chronic diarrhea, was losing weight, and was unable to hold

his food down. Buster had anemia and white gums, typical of advanced disease, and major hair loss, a side effect of the chemotherapy. A blood test revealed that the cat had serious hormonal imbalances affecting his immune system. He was producing killer cells that were not only attacking the leukemia virus but also his own tissue.

- Bob, a three-year-old mixed breed dog, and Cherry, a five-year-old shorthair female cat, shared the same household and the same daily diet of lamb and rice kibble. Their owner, like most people, believed that this type of diet was safe and hypoallergenic (hypoallergenic means the food does not cause allergic reactions). Yet, his dog and cat developed diarrhea and vomiting. Both animals had flaky skin and weight loss, signs of improper food absorption, and were clearly unhealthy. The concerned owner brought his pets to my clinic, puzzled over their illness.

- Candy had been a national field trial champion at the age of two, but a year later, the Brittany Spaniel refused to run, point, and fetch. She had been bred but could not conceive. Candy also developed "valley fever," a mysterious and hard-to-treat fungal condition that damages the lungs.

These cases are examples of an insidious, unsuspected epidemic that sickens, weakens, and kills companion animals before their time. Pure and mixed breeds, males and females, neutered, spayed, and intact animals: all are at risk. Because of this unrecognized epidemic, veterinarians are seeing an increase in the following:

- Cancer
- Autoimmune disorders
- Relentless skin allergies with inflammation, ulceration, and itchiness
- Severe hypersensitivity to food and insect bites
- Chronic bacterial, viral, and fungal infections
- Feline retroviruses and urinary syndrome
- Inflammatory bowel disease
- Inability to develop protective antibodies from vaccinations
- Obesity
- Miscarriages and sterility
- Aggressiveness and strange behavior
- Animals unresponsive to conventional treatment

- Chronic health problems among younger animals that previously affected mostly older animals
- Diseases among many breeds that were originally thought to affect only one particular breed

During more than thirty-five years in practice, I have treated tens of thousands of dogs and cats with these kinds of problems. Early on in my veterinary career, as I witnessed a parade of inexplicably sick animals brought to my clinic, I became dissatisfied with just treating the superficial signs of health problems. Too often the conventional treatments I trained for at veterinary school had little impact on pets seemingly more susceptible to disease and allergies and who seemed to be living shorter and sicker lives. I decided to investigate into the causes of sickness.

My clinical research led me to the discovery of a common underlying mechanism of imbalances within the endocrine and immune systems. Endocrine refers to the system of glands that produces hormones—protein molecules that serve as messengers in an amazing network of inner intelligence that regulates the body's function. Health and orderliness are based on this inner intelligence. There are myriad hormones made in the body, many of which scientists do not clearly understand. These substances are secreted by glands—such as the adrenals, ovaries, and thyroid—that are overseen by higher centers in the brain, namely the hypothalamus and pituitary.

The problem that I identified starts with hormonal imbalances that affect the immune system—the cells and organs that protect the body against bacteria, viruses, and disease. Specifically, a hormonal defect in the adrenal glands triggers a damaging domino effect among other hormones, weakening the immune system. The end result is a major loss of protection against disease and a greatly increased risk for disease.

Over time I found that many of the multiple problems I treated had the same common denominator of skewed hormones and compromised immune system. Some animals with this endocrine-immune disturbance developed clinical signs of disease early on in life. Others developed diseases later. I liken this disturbance to a timebomb. Some animals have long fuses, others short fuses. Sometimes the disturbance manifests dramatically in acute illness; other times, the endocrine-immune disturbance slowly unravels a healthy and orderly system, infecting the system with increasing chaos. In the process, animals are often unable to absorb medication and respond to conventional treatments. Until the imbalances are corrected, such treatments may not work.

Sometimes stress, poor diet, exposure to toxic chemicals, and parasites such as fleas can aggravate, or even cause the imbalances. However, my clinical studies indicate that animals are more likely to react to these factors simply because their immune systems are compromised by hormonal imbalances. For instance, itching and skin problems typically associated with fleas are usually secondary to hormonal-immune imbalances. Correct the imbalances and the animal becomes healthy. The fleas go elsewhere and target other weak animals.

Simply, the solution is to identify the hormonal defect and correct it. This is what I did for Georgette, Miles, Buster, Bob, Cherry, and Candy, all of whom recovered from their illnesses.

The therapy program includes the use of both natural and synthetic cortisone medication in a way that is extremely safe and effective. After years of successfully treating serious and chronic health problems, I am eager to share the rationale and guidelines for this program with pet owners and their veterinarians so they can similarly learn how to restore health to ailing dogs and cats.

I have seen the same imbalances create so much bad health and cut short so many lives, that I seriously fear for the survival of our cherished pets. The imbalances are found in animals globally even though most veterinarians do not know they exist. One thing is for sure: if this unrecognized epidemic continues to grow without proper recognition, identification, and treatment, the medical costs of maintaining pets may become so prohibitive that more and more people will opt out of the joy of having companion animals. The information in this book does not represent a cure-all by any stretch of the imagination, but it does represent an effective method to solve the cause of many of the common ailments of modern-day pets.

TWO

Clinical Evolution:
From Frustration to Discovery

In 1966, as I started my veterinary practice after completing veterinary school, I radiated brash professional confidence. Armed with the best training available and working knowledge of the latest surgical techniques and the most effective drugs, I was feeling invincible. Within a few years, however, it became quite clear that all my wonderful training was accomplishing very little healing.

Many of the dogs and cats brought in for treatment suffered from some sort of hypersensitivity such as itchy skin or overreaction to flea bites. Had I missed the boat in veterinary school? There had been no special emphasis on allergies or severe sensitivities, yet the volume of allergy traffic to my clinic was relentlessly high.

I treated the animals as taught, and referred to my textbooks and journals for extra assurance. I talked to veterinary school classmates and to more experienced veterinarians. Yes, I was doing it all in an acceptable manner, yet the results were mixed at best. Nothing seemed to work well. Animals would often benefit temporarily but problems would return sooner or later—and usually sooner.

Frustrated, I began to examine all the possibilities for allergy. There are only so many ways that allergens can enter the body and cause a reaction—through bites, direct contact through the skin, through inhaling, and through eating.

I gradually connected many cases directly to food sensitivities. I also began to realize that these sensitivities often did not just manifest as itchy skin, rashes, or gastrointestinal problems, but also as seemingly unrelated problems such as epilepsy, liver and kidney ailments, and other serious diseases. There was minimal research in the veterinary medical literature to guide me, so like a detective I searched for clues.

Foods and Allergies

One of the early eye-openers for me related to the quality—or rather, lack of it—of commercial pet food. Then, as now, intolerance to these diets is common. Intolerance can show up as violent sickness or chronic problems, and often trigger a hypersensitivity and overreaction to fleas and insect bites, soaps, sprays, and environmental contaminants.

Many mass-marketed pet foods are loaded with poor-quality ingredients derived from sources far from wholesome. This is definitely not fare fit for human consumption, and, in some cases not fit for your animal.

Pet food is convenience food and a huge industry has emerged in recent decades dedicated to supplying the growing number of companion animals. Today, feeding pets is megabusiness—more than $10 billion a year in sales.

According to a 1996 report by the Animal Protection Institute of America, more than 95 percent of our companion animals obtain their nutritional needs from a single source—highly processed commercial pet food.

"Our report clearly shows that what you purchase and what the manufacturers advertise are two entirely different products," states Alan Berger, president of the Institute. "The difference is threatening your animal's health, cutting short any chance of him enjoying old age, and maybe even killing him now. The ingredients they are using are not wholesome, and the harsh manufacturing practices that make those nifty little shapes, the ones our companion animals surely love to eat, destroy what little nutritional value the food ever had."

When author Ann Martin researched the quality of commercial pet food after her two dogs became ill in 1990 she was "absolutely horrified." She was so shocked, in fact, that she wrote an exposé, *Food Pets Die For: Shocking Facts About Pet Food* (NewSage Press, 1997, 2003). The pet food industry, she writes in this illuminating book, operates with virtually no government regulation and includes "deplorable" ingredients that can legally be used, such as euthanized dogs and cats, diseased cattle and horses, roadkill, dead zoo animals, and sawdust sweepings.

Ingredients are cooked up together and "manufactured" into food. Pesticides, hormone residues, and the euthanizing drugs survive the manufacturing process and are present in the bags and cans of pet food sold to consumers. Additives read like a who's who of food technology: anticaking, antimicrobial, coloring, firming, flavoring, drying, pH control, and surface finishing agents, as well as emulsifiers, sequestrants, synergists, texturizers, lubricants, and sweeteners.

Pet food manufacturers pay a good deal of attention to cosmetics. They want their pet food to look good so you will buy it even though animals could care less. In addition to all the gimmicky shapes, they use dyes that can actually make susceptible animals hyperactive: sodium nitrite to prevent fading of colors, or red dye #40 for a fresh meaty look. Both agents have long been linked to cancer or birth defects in laboratory animals, and in some countries are banned.

Manufacturers also put a lot of effort into taste. After all, they want animals to eat the stuff you buy so you will return to the store and buy more. Discarded restaurant grease, stabilized with powerful chemical antioxidants, is a favorite enhancer. Animals love the taste of fat.

Some products claim to cover the minimum daily nutritional requirements and are nothing more than that—minimum diets good only for minimum health. Some products do not even meet minimum standards. Even the term "minimum daily requirements" is misleading since this means little or nothing when considering what may be healthy for your pet.

Competition is fierce in the pet food market. Companies want your business and spend millions of dollars to get it with slick TV commercials, meaningless and misleading nutrition claims, and clever product names. In the competitive scramble, quality and good nutrition are often sacrificed to economics and profit. Quality can change even within single product lines of a company. Manufacturers constantly seek cheaper ingredients to replace more expensive ones.

Pet owners have the well being of their animals at heart but they also want to feed their animals conveniently and cheaply. Often, they will feed the same restricted diet without change, month after month. But feeding conveniently and cheaply may cost more in the long run—in veterinary bills. Cheap food means cheap ingredients. A diet of poor-quality ingredients, fed without variation over a length of time, has the potential to promote deficiencies, malabsorption, sensitivities, and a reduced ability to cope with environmental stresses such as fleas.

Animals may become fatter, develop skin problems, mood swings, and an array of health disorders.

If the pet food picture appears bleak, do not be discouraged. There are options. Health-conscious consumers have been demanding better quality food. Fortunately, segments of the industry have responded in recent years to this growing demand. A lot of poor quality products are still available, but there are improved natural pet foods on the market. In general, higher quality pet foods can be found at health food stores. Of course, the best option is to prepare fresh and wholesome meals for your pet at home. But home preparation is a time commitment and many busy people may not have the time. Also, keep in mind that a sensitive animal can have a reaction to a specific food, whether it is fresh and organic or part of a multi-ingredient kibble. I discuss this, and other feeding issues, in greater detail in Chapter Six and Chapter Ten.

Early on in my practice I began to design dietary strategies and home-cooked recipes to help my clients deal with the challenge of feeding their pets a healthy and non-allergenic diet. I found that about 30 percent of the animals improved partially or wholly on modified diets in which we eliminated certain antagonistic foods. My clients appreciated the improved health of their animals but some complained about the extra work and time involved in preparing special diets. One annoyed client called to protest about the half-hour he just spent peeling carrots for his dogs. His feedback motivated me to develop a frozen-loaf, non-meat product for pets that I called "Naturally Yours." It contained soybeans, brown rice, carrots, and celery. Because I wanted to avoid preservatives, I used water in the recipe as a preservative by freezing the loaf. It worked great. Several years later, however, I learned that some animals with the endocrine-immune problem became intolerant of soybeans after they were exposed to this food for a period of time.

In the early 1980s I formulated a number of diets for a new company called Nature's Recipe that was interested in bringing higher quality pet food to the marketplace. (Note that the original owners of Nature's Recipe sold the company in 1996 to H. J. Heinz Company.) As part of that activity I developed the first lamb and rice formula designed to be a healthy hypoallergenic alternative for the ubiquitous beef- and chicken- based formulas which I found caused allergic reactions in many sensitive animals. This may come as a surprise to you but today, because of the subsequent proliferation of lamb and rice formulas, the combination is no longer the same reliable hypoallergenic feeding option. I talk more about this in Chapter Six.

In the early years I turned up still another major health clue related to food. I found that many animals lack the digestive enzyme "firepower" to break down highly complex diets, particularly kibble. The result: an inability to properly process food. This problem in turn created nutritional shortfalls that lead to allergic-like reactions and disease. With time and growing clinical experience, I calculated that about half of the animals I treated had problems related specifically to food and digestion. In Chapter Eleven, I explain how to increase an animal's digestive powers with a simple nutritional supplement.

Along with concern about better feeding techniques, my early clinical work led me to a fascinating trail of hormonal imbalances. These imbalances appear to be caused in large part by the way animals are bred.

The Ravages of Overbreeding

The history of pet breeding practices is filled with bad news—animals with gross deformities, lost instincts, altered and bizarre behavior, and multiple health disorders.

The problem stems in large part from rampant linebreeding and inbreeding. Linebreeding refers to mating animals in the same family. Inbreeding means mating closely related animals with genetically similar constitutions.

These breeding practices are aimed at creating certain looks, colors, and physical criteria that win ribbons at dog and cat shows. Such honors translate into fashionable and trendy "products" and the merchandising of blue-blood offspring at inflated prices. Following the trends, puppy and kitty mills churn out "designer pets," often using abusive, disgraceful assembly line methods.

Although fashionable and beautiful on the surface, inside these animals are frequently damaged goods, suffering from physiological defects that render them unhealthy and less able to cope with life.

I did not know any of this when I started out as a veterinarian. We were not taught about breeding fallout in veterinary school. But as I treated and observed more animals, I began to find unmistakable patterns of hypersensitivity and disease among littermates and along familial lines. I treated many offspring of father-daughter, mother-son, and sibling matings with inflamed skin, ulcerations, itchiness, malabsorption, and internal systems out of control.

Unfortunately, these breeding practices have continued over the years and intensified. In 1994, *Time* magazine dedicated a cover story to the problem, calling it "the shame of overbreeding." Most popular dog breeds have been bred "almost exclusively to look good," the article states, and this "obsessive focus on show-ring looks is crippling, sometimes fatally, America's purebred dogs."

Time notes that that there are more than 300 different genetic disorders that may subject animals to enormous pain and suffering. "The astonishing thing," the magazine article reports, "is that despite the scope of these diseases, veterinary researchers know next to nothing about what causes them or how to cure them."

Since the publication of the *Time* article, research into genetically based diseases of dogs and cats has increased significantly. Although much has been learned, researchers admit that long-term management of these diseases still remains difficult.

Breeding practices have depleted the hardiness and function of many dogs and cats. Animals chosen to perpetuate the popular appearance of a specific breed carry very similar genes. Nature, the ultimate supervisor of animal breeding, succeeds only with varied gene pools. With a diverse genetic code for a species, Nature assures itself that weaker qualities will not perpetuate across generations. But with the meddling of human hands, weaker attributes have become entrenched and perpetuated in narrower and narrower gene pools. For instance, dog breeders scramble to clarify the cosmetic features that enable them to register their animals as separate breeds with the American Kennel Club.

Increasingly, damaged dogs are being sold to unsuspecting buyers. I have seen sobbing children carry in the casualties—helpless and pathetic young animals, sometimes with oozing sores all over their bodies, sometimes hairless and emaciated, sometimes so weak they can not stand, and sometimes with all of these signs.

The costs in terms of heartbreak, suffering, and veterinary bills are immense. Veterinarians are faced with chaotic conditions they are unable to resolve. Moreover, each generation of animals seems to be more susceptible to illness.

The genetic fallout of poor health is seen not only with purebreds, but also among mixed breeds from the pound or shelter. They harbor and perpetuate the purebred defects in their blood. Thus, diseases once considered specific to certain breeds are now widely established in other breeds and in mixed breeds.

The genetic crisis among pets includes obvious structural and sensory flaws. Prime examples are deafness among Dalmatians, vision defects among Collies, and underdeveloped tracheas in English Bulldogs, which predispose them to choking. Among cats, you have Persians with nasal discharges and constant snuffles from breeding for a pushed-in face, and tailless Manx with rear leg mobility problems.

Less appreciated is the impact that genetic flaws can have on basic biological functioning—hormone production is one example. In my early clinical investigations, I was fortunate enough to discover one such defect that results in a ripple effect of chaos throughout the immune system. With this discovery, which I explain in the next chapter, came a remarkable diagnostic and therapeutic program that has helped thousands of animals suffering from many common disorders.

THREE

Endocrine-Immune Chaos: Putting the Puzzle Together

In 1969 a medical research laboratory contracted me to inspect their animal-testing environment. Instead of a fee I asked the laboratory to run antibody levels on blood samples drawn from my patients. No other veterinarians I knew did this kind of testing but I thought such measurements might help me figure out how effectively the immune system was operating. Immune system cells called B cells produce nine different classes of antibodies, which are like protein "missiles" that identify and/or destroy harmful substances entering the body. Such foreign invaders include viruses, bacteria, fungi, and parasites. Antibodies are also known as immunoglobulins. I asked the laboratory to measure five of them: immunoglobulin A (IgAl), immunoglobulin D (IgD), immunoglobulin E (IgE), immunoglobulin G (IgG), and immunoglobulin M (IgM).

It took about two years before I was able to confidently define healthy and unhealthy ranges for what appeared to be the most significant antibodies related to pathogens and to the many cases of hypersensitivity I observed in dogs and cats. The relevant antibodies were IgG, IgM, and, in particular, IgA.

IgA concentrations are found in great abundance in mucous membranes, such as the linings of the respiratory, gastrointestinal, and urinary tracts. There these antibodies perform major sentry duty and keep undesirable microorganisms from reaching the deep tissues and organs of the body. IgG and IgM are important interceptors operating in the bloodstream.

I first applied my new standard of antibody ranges in 1972 to the case of a sick Golden Retriever puppy named Sunshine. The poor dog suffered from acute hypersensitivity to food that caused his ears and muzzle to become severely swollen, bloody, and inflamed. His face had the appearance of raw hamburger meat. Analysis of his blood sample showed antibody levels quite low.

I prescribed 5 milligrams daily of Prednisolone, a cortisone medication, to reduce the inflammation, and an antibiotic to handle the bacteria. (I now use Prednisone.) Within a few days the dog was much better. I retested for antibody levels and was shocked. The levels were clearly improved from the baseline test before treatment. How could this occur? I indeed expected the anti-inflammatory effect. After all, physicians and veterinarians have long used highly effective cortisone drugs short-term to combat allergic reactions and relieve conditions involving inflammation and itching. These medications, frequently called steroids, are important therapeutic drugs. Cortisone, a catch-all term for the various forms of this family of drugs, is the pharmaceutical equivalent of cortisol, an important hormone produced by the adrenal glands that exerts a potent anti-inflammatory effect in the body. But everybody knows that cortisone suppresses immune cells. So why did the antibodies increase in Sunshine's case? I was puzzled.

I started poring over physiology and endocrinology books seeking an explanation. I found some basic information, but no specific explanation for the improvement in antibody levels.

I then wondered if a genetic defect was somehow at work causing a problem with the natural output of cortisol by the adrenal glands, and this, in turn, was having a negative effect on the immune system. Could breeding practices create cortisol defective or deficient animals who are unable to adequately defend themselves against allergens, microorganisms, and disease?

I also wondered if veterinarians, unaware of such a possible genetic flaw, could inadvertently be compensating for it—at least in the short term—with the routine use of cortisone drugs that so effectively relieve common inflammation. In other words, was the cortisone acting not just as a medicine but as a hormone replacement?

A friend of mine, Arnold Epstein, was a partner in a major veterinary diagnostic laboratory that did the blood work for my cases. I asked him to start checking the cortisol levels of my patients plagued with chronic allergies. The tests consistently produced low cortisol values. In addition, antibody levels were low. When I treated these patients with cortisone, as I had with Sunshine, the antibody levels normalized, and the animals improved.

I suspected that cortisol had a regulating influence on the immune system. If cortisol was low, as it was in these sick animals, then the immune system apparently became weakened or destabilized in some way, resulting in low antibody levels. When I replaced the apparently missing or defective cortisol with cortisone, the antibody levels came right back up and the animals improved. Maybe a genetic defect was at work, causing chaos in the adrenal cortex, where cortisol is made.

However, I was concerned with how long I could keep such defective animals on cortisone. I was certainly aware of the well-documented side effects of cortisone drugs and the general reluctance of doctors to use these medications on a long-term basis. Such reluctance exists to this very day. Among the common fears is suppression of the immune system. In fact, cortisone drugs are prescribed for immune suppression against certain diseases.

I obviously had no wish to suppress the immune function of animals whose immune systems might be destabilized nor did I want to create any side effects. As a possible solution I tried prescribing low dosages of cortisone, well below the standard therapeutic levels. This was appropriate, I reasoned, if my strategy was to replace a deficient hormone on a long-term basis rather than apply the medication conventionally for temporary relief of clinical signs. The low-dosage scheme worked fine for cats but after a while I noticed signs of overdosing in some dogs. Such signs included listlessness and increased drinking, appetite and urination, and panting at night. I also noticed that the continued usage of cortisone in dogs, even at a low dosage, was causing antibody levels to dip again in an unhealthy direction.

Looking for clues, I went back to the books again. I came across some information about androgens and estrogens that are produced in the adrenal glands. I decided to look into this. Androgens are hormones primarily associated with the masculine gender, such as testosterone and dehydroepiandrosterone (DHEA), however they are also produced by females. In turn, males also produce some estrogen, the female sex hormone. I wondered if the cortisol problem could somehow be related to estrogen and androgens coming out of the adrenals. I then started asking the laboratory for estrogen and androgen measurements in my experimental blood workups.

After I started an animal on cortisone and retested blood levels, I found that the concentration of estrogen dropped from a pre-treatment level. I saw this pattern over and over in sick animals whether they were cats or dogs, males or females, neutered or intact. Thus there was an estrogen effect going on that could not be explained by ovarian activity but was in some way connected to the cortisol. Moreover, I found a similar pattern with the androgen level in dogs and cats of both sexes. If there was a cortisol problem, the androgen level was initially higher and, after the start of cortisone therapy, it was lower. The results were fascinating but I could not immediately figure out the meaning.

I then decided to look at the thyroid gland because I was finding that many of my sick dogs had signs of hypothyroidism—low thyroid function. The thyroid gland, located in the neck, produces hormones that regulate metabolism, the chemical processes occurring within the cells of an organism necessary for the maintenance of life. The signs of low thyroid function I observed in the dogs included slower than normal heart rate, lower than normal body temperature, higher than normal levels of cholesterol and triglycerides, and lethargy and bilateral hair loss. This was occurring despite the fact that the thyroid hormone levels usually appeared normal in blood tests. In the face of these normal results I still opted to give the dogs thyroid medication. I found that the clinical signs of low thyroid then improved.

In 1976, Broda Barnes, M.D., explained in his landmark book *Hypothyroidism: The Unsuspected Illness* (Harper & Row) that low thyroid function and symptoms could occur even though standard blood tests show the thyroid hormone levels to be normal. I did not know this at the time I was struggling with my own clinical research. I also did not know that high estrogen can bind thyroid hormones, that is, render them inactive in part, and thus interfere with their actions. This binding effect on thyroid, I later learned, does not show up on standard blood tests. I also learned that the estrogen-binding effect could possibly be significant enough to hamper thyroid activity, and maybe slow down the metabolism and the ability to process the cortisone.

I began treating dogs simultaneously with cortisone and thyroid hormone. Now I found that not only did the estrogen level decrease and the antibodies increase, as before, but the antibody levels remained at a healthy level even with the continued cortisone therapy. There were no more signs of cortisone overdose. Canine patients improved and stayed healthy as long as the therapy was maintained. The dogs now seemed to process the cortisone effectively and disallow any kind of toxic buildup that might be occurring due to a thyroid problem. Cats, for some species-specific variation, needed only the cortisone, without thyroid, in the vast majority of cases.

I also tested for T cell levels and found them also consistently low. T cells are major players in the immune system. Some are involved in the complex orchestration of the body's multiple immune factors, including activation of the B cells that produce antibodies. Others destroy infected cells directly. For example, they help eliminate cells infected by viruses or cells taken over by cancer.

For the better part of a year I paid for all this testing out of my own pocket because I felt the research was experimental. Until I felt confident that I could use the testing procedure to accurately assess the endocrine-immune problem and measure the progress of the therapy, I did not charge my clients.

I eventually chose to drop the T cell and androgen measurements from the blood test because of their significant added cost. I settled on cortisol, estrogen, thyroid, and antibody activity as my basic endocrine-immune status indicators. These factors provided an excellent yardstick and a combination that was readily affordable for my clients.

Within a year I had put together enough of the puzzle to give me a working understanding of an otherwise unrecognized endocrine-immune disturbance and a good program with which to effectively test it and correct it. Sunshine was the first beneficiary. He regained his health and lived to the ripe age of seventeen on a lifelong maintenance program of low-dosage cortisone and thyroid. The adrenal defect he had apparently inherited was corrected by this approach. Instead of a miserable and probable short life, Sunshine thrived and lived up to his name.

Anatomy of an Endocrine-Immune Defect

Over the years I have continued to refine my program and understand further the fine points of the disease mechanism I have uncovered. On the following pages is an overview as I see it today.

The problem starts in the two adrenal glands, located adjacent to the kidneys. In a large dog each kidney is the size of two side-by-side

The Adrenal Gland

ADRENAL GLAND
KIDNEY
ESOPHAGUS
COLON
TRACHEA
RECTUM
STOMACH
ANUS
LUNGS
SMALL INTESTINE
HEART
SPLEEN
LIVER

Cross-section of Adrenal

CORTEX
ZONA GLOMERULOSA
MEDULLA
ZONA FASCICULATA
INTERFACE LAYER?
ZONA RETICULARIS

silver dollars; in a cat or small dog, it is the size of two almonds. And there, just forward of each kidney is the tiny thumbnail-shaped adrenal gland that produces an array of important hormones.

Each adrenal gland has two basic parts: a central core called the medulla that produces the well-known stress hormone adrenaline, and a surrounding ring of outer tissue, the cortex, that secretes cortisol and other important hormones.

The adrenal hormones are best known for their role in protecting people and animals alike from life's constant stresses—major or minor.

Governed by higher centers in the brain, adrenal and other hormones are protein chemical messengers carrying powerful commands that basically operate the physiology. Life itself is based on this inner communication. Dispatched as needed by the brain, hormonal secretions travel through the bloodstream to the body's trillions of cells. On outer and inner membranes of the cells are receptor sites that function like locks on a door. In order to get in and tell the DNA what to do, the right key is needed. Hormones are the keys. They travel from glands to specific target cells, unlock the receptor sites, and deliver their biochemical message for processing. They turn on or turn off specific cellular functions, and measure cellular activity throughout the system.

The cortex is a veritable factory of steroid hormones, compounds with a particular chemical structure that are derived from cholesterol. The outer layer of the cortex called the zona glomerulosa produces aldosterone, a hormone that regulates potassium and sodium levels in the body, critical for proper nerve reaction and muscular activity. The middle layer (zona fasciculata) produces cortisol. The inner layer (zona reticularis) secretes the androgen hormones dehydroepiandrosterone (DHEA) and dehydroepiandrosterone sulfate (DHEAS). There may also be an "interface" layer in the cortex that produces estrogen.

Cortisol is known to be the primary secretory product of the adrenal glands in dogs and humans. Best known as a stress hormone, cortisol also provides many other services in the body. It prompts certain biochemical activities that increase and normalize blood sugar levels when they drop too low. Scientists recognize that a profound loss of cortisol can lead to a critical state of deranged metabolism and an inability to deal with stress and infections.

Cortisol, as I mentioned earlier, is also a powerful anti-inflammatory agent. This particular property was the inspiration for the research and development of cortisone drugs, a family of pharmaceutical versions of cortisol. The 1950 Nobel Prize in physiology and medicine was awarded to the scientists who first synthesized cortisone and applied it clinically for rheumatoid arthritis, a highly inflammatory condition. Today, cortisone drugs are widely used around the world in both human and veterinary medicine.

As a medication used at powerful pharmacologic dosages, cortisone preparations also have strong immunosuppressive activity. They are frequently applied to suppress the immune system in autoimmune diseases where the body's defenses attack the body's own tissue.

In my research I have learned that at a basal, or normal level, the body's own cortisol exerts a very discriminating regulatory effect on molecular "mediators" that turn on or turn off activity related to immunity and inflammation. It is a very complex business. The bottom line is that a normal level of cortisol seems to be required for a normal immune response. A deficiency of cortisol may result in an unresponsive immune system, whereas too much cortisone medication or too much of the body's own active cortisol suppresses immune responses. An excess of active cortisol or cortisone drugs can lead to a condition known as Cushing's syndrome. In Cushing's, individuals develop severe fatigue, weak muscles, high blood pressure, high blood sugar, and fertility and menstrual problems, among other symptoms.

Cortisol deficiency, the other side of the coin, tends to be overlooked in medical circles. A deficiency or ineffectiveness of cortisol certainly appears to cause many problems. I have seen this consistently in animals. Compared to healthy animals, I have found that sick and diseased pets often have too little cortisol, or the cortisol present is somehow in a bound or ineffective state, resulting in systemic imbalances and chaos throughout the physiology. The particular problem I see does not relate to Addison's disease, a condition involving a deficiency of aldosterone, the hormone governing sodium and potassium levels in the body, and which is produced in the outer cortex layer of the adrenal glands. I have not found low levels of aldosterone in cortisol-deficient patients nor have I seen any of the typical signs of Addison's. In humans, cortisol deficiency has been linked to chronic fatigue, allergies, rheumatoid arthritis, and lowered resistance to infections. I discuss this in more detail in Chapter Sixteen.

The pituitary gland, a pea-sized organ located at the base of the brain, governs cortisol release with a hormone called adrenocorticotropin or ACTH. This substance prods the adrenal cortex into production when the circulating cortisol level is too low. ACTH also applies the brakes when there is too much cortisol circulating. In turn, a hormone manufactured in the hypothalamus region of the brain oversees the ACTH activity. This hormone is called corticotropic-releasing factor (CRF).

Thus, cortisol secretion is suppressed or stimulated by "feedback loops." When blood concentrations rise above a certain threshold, the circulating cortisol inhibits the hypothalamus-pituitary axis. This then inhibits ACTH and cortisol secretion. When the adrenal gland is unable to produce enough cortisol, or for some reason the cortisol is "bound," or otherwise inactive, and thus not recognized by the system, the hypothalamus and pituitary respond by calling for more cortisol.

This activity goes on automatically in the body. The interaction is like a thermostat that turns the heat on when the temperature drops below a certain level and then cuts off again when the temperature rises. The hypothalamus-pituitary-adrenal relationship is just one of many finely tuned feedback mechanisms within the endocrine system. While it is now recognized that this network, as part of the neuroendocrine system, has central importance to immune function, researchers still admit to a lack of clear understanding about the countless details and interactions.

Healthy Adrenal-Immune Relationships

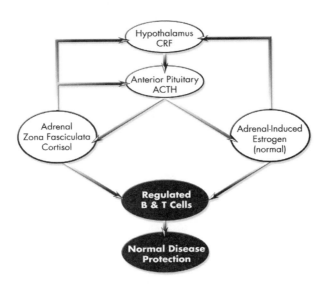

The hypothalamus and pituitary monitor the cortisol level and prompt the adrenal cortex to produce more, or less, as needed. The primary immune system cells are working normally and provide protection against disease.

Genetic Defects from Breeding

Humans have created innumerable defects and health problems among companion animals by genetically manipulating the physical attributes of different breeds. Breeders' visions of external perfection have led to profound internal imperfection. My clinical research has shown that among the problems of overbreeding is a major corruption of the cortisol system. Specifically, the middle layer of the adrenal cortex where cortisol is produced appears to have been damaged. The domino effect that follows has seriously corrupted the natural mechanisms connecting the endocrine and the immune systems. Many animals cannot produce enough cortisol, or what they do produce is largely inactive. Other hormones are thrown out of balance as a result. The flaws are passed down from generation to generation, from purebreds to purebreds, from purebreds to mixed breeds, and from mixed breeds to other mixed breeds.

Many years ago I did an extended series of routine autopsies on predominantly purebred animals of all ages after they had succumbed to illness. I removed and carefully examined the adrenal glands in both dogs and cats. In most cases I found that the adrenal cortex was visibly smaller than normal to the naked eye. Under closer scrutiny with the microscope I often found grossly underdeveloped cortical tissue with a lack of cellular solidity and structure. Frequently I found inflamed, congested, and hemorrhaged tissue in the cortex.

Veterinary pathologists have reported the existence of varying degrees of abnormal adrenal cortical tissue but have apparently never related this to classic adrenal diseases and never directly to any signs of illness. In humans, some evidence suggests that such tissue alteration may be a result from bacterial infections, prolonged cortisone therapy, or autoimmune attack on the adrenal glands.

Not all of the autopsies revealed shrunken, abnormal tissue. I also found normal-looking glands in cortisol-deficient animals I had tested when they were alive. So the defect was not always visibly apparent. There could be some problem, such as a genetic lack of certain enzymes necessary for the complete production of cortisol. But the problem was real, and animals were profoundly diseased, whether the defect was visible or not.

The Estrogen Connection: A Double Whammy

One of the consistent measurements of endocrine-immune imbalances is elevated estrogen. We all think of estrogen as the female sex hormone produced in the ovaries, but estrogen can also come from other sources in the body of humans and animals, including the adrenal glands. Thus, estrogen is present in males as well as females without ovaries.

More than 90 percent of the cases I treat involve neutered or spayed animals. Thus, in the case of most female dogs and cats I see, there is no influence of ovarian estrogen. Among the females with intact ovaries, I test for imbalances when animals are not in estrus and therefore not producing a high level of ovarian estrogen.

When the zona fasciculata cannot make enough cortisol, or for some reason the cortisol is excessively bound (inactive) or defective, and thus not recognized by the system, the pituitary continues to release ACTH in order to stimulate more cortisol. This results in elevated estrogen in the system. There are two possible explanations for this:

1) The zona reticularis of the adrenal cortex also responds to ACTH. This is where the androgen hormones DHEA and DHEAS are made. They are the most abundant circulating hormones in the body and are known as prohormones in that they convert into other hormones. Through enzymatic actions, they can convert to androstenedione, androstenediol, testosterone, and further to the estrogen compounds estrone and estradiol in other tissues of the body, such as muscle and fat. Androstenedione is the most important precursor of estrone, while androstenediol has inherent estrogenic activity.

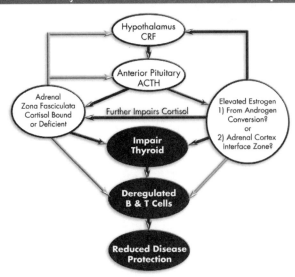

This diagram depicts a cascade of chaos emanating from the adrenal cortex. The defect starts with insufficient or defective cortisol. The hypothalamus and pituitary respond by releasing more ACTH, but the cortex is unable to produce enough cortisol or what it produces is defective. The flow of ACTH continues, promoting an adrenally-based release of male and female hormones, leading to destabilization of thyroid and immune function.

2) Some researchers say that an interface, or transition zone, of tissue between the zona fasciculata and reticularis of the adrenal cortex is capable of directly producing sex hormones, including estrogen compounds. This concept first appeared in a 1969 book, *Functional Pathology of the Human Adrenal Gland* (E & S. Livingstone, Ltd), written by Thomas Symington, a professor of pathology at the University of Glasgow. In a 1999 article in the journal *Biochemical Pharmacology*, Eugene Roberts, a City of Hope neurobiochemist, also suggested that these "interface cells" manufacture testosterone, estrone, and estradiol.

As a busy clinical practitioner and not a medical researcher I have not had the means to investigate the actual source of non-ovarian estrogen. I only know that I find elevated estrogen in my sick patients and that the level drops when I start cortisone replacement. Whatever the source, this element of estrogen is physiologically significant. It adds to the chaos in the cortex and elsewhere. The potential for problems is evident from the following information:

- Studies in humans have shown that estrogens interfere with the enzyme activity needed to synthesize cortisol in the adrenal cortex. Thus, if there were a cortisol defect to begin with, added estrogen would appear to aggravate the situation and worsen the overall imbalance.
- Excess estrogen turns on the hypothalamus in the brain. The hypothalamus governs the pituitary. Too little cortisol causes the hypothalamus to command the pituitary to produce more adrenal-stimulating ACTH. Too much estrogen does the same thing. The hypothalamus releases its corticotropic-releasing factor (CRF). The pituitary responds by producing more ACTH. The ACTH performs its mission by rushing to the adrenal gland where it gets little or no response from the middle layer of the cortex. In the process, ACTH stirs up the inner layer and causes the release of more estrogen. If an interface zone exists, it too appears to respond to ACTH and may release sex hormones.
- Too much estrogen causes tiny blood vessels to become more permeable. This is a histamine-like effect, and allows blood components to spill into adjacent tissue, causing inflammation and irritation.

- At higher and pharmacological concentrations, estrogens have inhibitory actions on the immune system. For instance, elevated estrogen is associated with atrophy of the thymus gland, an important organ located in the chest area where immune cells undergo a maturation process. The destabilization and weakening of immune system function that I see in animals is consistently associated with low cortisol and elevated estrogen.

- I find elevated estrogen part of the endocrine-immune imbalance in dogs and cats with autoimmune conditions. Among humans, recent data indicate that increased estrogen levels may trigger autoimmune diseases. (See Chapter Sixteen.)

- High estrogen can impact the thyroid—specifically binding and inactivating thyroid hormones. Because the thyroid regulates cellular metabolism, efficiency can suffer as a result, and the system may slow down. Most doctors and veterinarians are not aware of the estrogen connection contributing to signs of low thyroid. A veterinarian will test the amount of thyroid hormones in the blood and usually find the level normal. However, the problem is that these hormones may be in a "bound" or inactive state.

- Excess estrogen suppresses bone marrow activity that includes the manufacture of red blood cells. Anemia can result.

The Bottom Line

In the fifty plus years since they first appeared in the medical marketplace, the pharmaceutical derivatives of cortisol—that is, cortisone (steroid) compounds—have had a huge presence because of their clinically important anti-inflammatory and immune suppression applications. During this time we have learned a great deal also about the side effects of these compounds when used at typically powerful, pharmacologic dosages. For that reason steroids are usually prescribed for short-term use and, despite their medical importance, have acquired a tarnished reputation. Medical doctors and veterinarians shy away from using cortisone on a long-term basis because of the widespread fear of side effects and suppressing the immune system.

This development has obscured interest in the pivotal physiologic roles of cortisol and applications of low-dosage cortisone as a "hormone replacement" for cortisol deficiency. In Chapter Sixteen, I describe how medical doctors are increasingly finding long-term, low-dosage corti-sone safe and effective, and how one doctor has been using this approach for decades to help patients with a cortisol deficiency who suffer from allergies, chronic fatigue, and rheumatoid arthritis.

In animals with healthy adrenals, sustained cortisone medication indeed has the potential to suppress the immune system and cause side effects because too much cortisol and cortisone are then present in the body. Remember that cortisone compounds convert in the body to cortisol. This is why treatment with potent, pharmacologic amounts of cortisone often has no long-lasting benefits and leads to problems. But in an animal with defective adrenals, cortisone at the proper low-dosage level does wonders. It may, in fact, be the only thing that can save the lives of very sick animals.

My clinical practice and research have shown that the conservative use of cortisone makes up for the shortage in animals with an impaired ability to produce healthy amounts of cortisol. The replacement cortisone slows down ACTH, as would naturally happen if the animal had adequate cortisol. This in turn stops the influx of unwanted extra estrogen. With cortisone now substituting for missing cortisol and with estrogen lowered, orderliness returns to the immune system allowing immune cells to protect the body.

A second, and important element in the therapy, is the concurrent use of thyroid hormone replacement. I have found this to be a necessity in all canine cases, and in about 10 percent of feline cases. In Chapter Nine, I detail the precise treatment for hormonal replacement. The information is intended primarily to guide veterinarians in the use of low-dosage cortisol replacement therapy for maximum health benefits without side effects.

The endocrine-immune disturbance I have identified seriously compromises the ability of animals to protect themselves against disease. Hormones have gone awry and collectively undermined the intelligence, stability and potency of the immune system. There are many possible combinations for malfunction and disease because there are many possible combinations and degrees of imbalances in the countless endocrine connections. I do not understand all the molecular details involved. And I do not know anyone who does. I only know that the imbalances I measure in my animals are real and that they cause real problems. I also know how to repair the imbalances.

Long-Term Hormone Replacement Therapy Restores Balance and Health to Previously Imbalanced Endocrine-Immune Pets

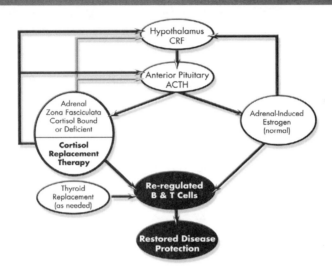

At first, the imbalances may cause a minor problem, such as allergic dermatitis, a hot spot, a reaction to a vaccine, or a reaction to a fleabite. But as time goes on, the underlying disorder can spawn more serious problems—such as autoimmunity and cancer—and contribute to an early death. I have also seen affected animals develop catastrophic diseases right from the start that may not be treatable. Examples: dogs with a fatal cancer called hemangio sarcoma, or cats with severe skin cancer.

In the next two chapters I describe some of the many conditions where the endocrine-immune imbalances cause illness.

– FOUR –

Imbalanced Dogs

Years ago, veterinarians associated certain breeds with susceptibility for developing certain illnesses. For instance, Doberman Pinschers developed Von Willebrand's disease, a blood-clotting disorder. English Cockers had a volatile temperament. Chronic ear infections were common to Cockers, Beagles, and Standard Poodles. Today, the situation is different. Many conditions that once appeared confined to particular breeds have jumped the fence, so to speak, and no longer conform to breed boundaries. They now tend to affect all canines—from aristocratic purebreds to the most humble of mixed breeds.

Unless somebody puts forward a better explanation, I believe this proliferation of genetic-based disorders may have a common underlying cause: endocrine-immune imbalances. There appears to be a similar pattern of imbalances present in sick animals from all breeds. Some have it more seriously, others less so. Based on personal consultations with veterinarians, breeders, rescue organizations, and pet owners internationally, this is not just a U.S. problem. The disorder is global.

The particular aspect of an animal's health that is affected is different for each animal. Endocrine-immune imbalances may cause a skin condition, a super sensitivity to fleas, a failure to develop immunity after vaccination, inflammatory bowel disease, or cancer. Sometimes the imbalances manifest as strange or aggressive behavior. There are breed groups and breeders extremely concerned because their animals are inundated with cancer and autoimmune problems.

In many cases, the endocrine-immune imbalance causes a general decline in vitality and resistance. Animals develop multiple signs of illness and at an earlier age than ever before. In the past, Great Pyrenees and other large breeds lived twelve or fourteen years. Now breeders say many of these animals are dying much earlier, some as young as two and three. Today, a big dog living to seven or eight years old is practically an exception to the rule. Some breeders acknowledge a genetic crisis but do not know what to do about it. Unfortunately, other breeders do not even want to admit there is a problem.

For years I treated a beautiful black Great Dane with the auspicious name of Roquefort Goldberg. He had major problems but on a good hormone replacement program and a supportive diet he lived a healthy life and died at fifteen. And that is the case for most of my big patients. They live healthy lives as long as their human companions keep them on the program.

These examples are only the tip of the iceberg. In this chapter I chronicle a broad selection of conditions in which the endocrine-immune defect works insidiously, hidden from view, as a reaper of destruction and misery. If the mechanism is not identified and remedied, it continues to sow the seeds of sickness and death despite all the good efforts of veterinarians.

Allergies

After the publication of my book *Pet Allergies: Remedies for an Epidemic* in 1986, many veterinarians contacted me to learn more details about endocrine-immune imbalances and the solution of hormone replacement. I have been gratified to hear back from many of them with reports of significant success in dealing with a widespread and challenging pet health problem. The sight of dogs constantly scratching or chewing on their skin drives pet owners to distraction—and to veterinary clinics *en masse* for help. The causes are many, including fleabite sensitivities, food or airborne allergens, reactions to vaccinations, and chemicals in the environment. But the connection between allergies and cortisol deficiency with too much estrogen is still unrecognized by most of the veterinary community.

Medical dictionaries define an allergy as "a hypersensitive state acquired through exposure to a particular allergen." An allergen is any substance that can cause an immediate or delayed reaction. Such substances include pollen, dust, mold, food, chemicals, insect bites, and fleabites.

My definition of allergies is as follows: A hypersensitive state either inherited or acquired that can cause everyday scratching problems but serious and even fatal disease as well.

On a daily basis I see animals with inferior or damaged immunity seriously affected by environmental input. I have long believed that an unrecognized allergy epidemic ruins the health of millions of animals and seriously threatens their survival. And since I wrote my first book, the situation has only gotten worse. Perhaps one out of two animals brought to veterinary hospitals may be suffering from some degree of allergic malady. Allergies are so common that most pet owners will likely face the problem one time or another during the life of their animals.

Humans sniffle, sneeze, cough, and wheeze when they are insulted by an allergen. Dogs most frequently itch and scratch. The difference has to do with mast cells, specialized cells in the body that respond to allergens by producing a chemical called histamine. Histamine then triggers symptoms by causing small blood vessels to leak and ooze fluid, resulting in a swelling of tissue. In humans, mast cells are highly concentrated in the area of the eyes, nose, and windpipe. That is why, for instance, people with hayfever experience nasal congestion. It is the result of leaky vessels and swelling in the nose.

In animals, mast cells are concentrated on the sides of the face, paws, armpits, and groin. And that is why affected pets rub their faces, lick their feet, and scratch their armpits and groins incessantly.

But allergic reactions are not just limited to disturbances on the surface. There can be multiple signs of physical and behavioral symptoms. Skin is indeed affected most frequently but intestinal disorders, behavioral disturbances, seizures, and other problems also occur, both with or without a parallel skin problem.

Many new clients tell me their dogs continually lick the skin and cause open sores. "It's because the dog is bored and has nothing to do all day while we are away at work," they say. Not true, in my opinion. Lick granuloma, as the problem is called, is more likely a sign of the endocrine defect at work, and probably food allergies as well.

New allergies can arise any time an animal is exposed to any substance for a period of time. Some allergic reactions appear after exposure to a single allergen, others after exposure to multiple substances. It depends on an animal's individual resistance.

Cortisone has long been used to help allergies of many types. Patients are often much better because of the medication. But cortisone is thought to be a dangerous medication with the potential to create many side effects. This is indeed true at typically potent pharmacologic dosages. But at smaller, physiologic dosages there is great potential to heal and maintain strong protection against allergy susceptibility for a lifetime. My approach to chronic allergies in pets starts with a test to determine endocrine-immune imbalances. (See Chapter Eight.) If the irregularities are present I can safely go ahead with cortisone replacement on a physiologic basis. In most canine cases, I also provide thyroid replacement for the long haul.

The thyroid connection is important in dogs and usually overlooked. A cortisol deficiency and resultant increase in estrogen can both bind up and interfere with thyroid hormones to some degree. This can slow down the metabolism, including the body's ability to break down and detoxify not only the burden of allergens but also the hormone replacement—in this case, cortisone. Therapy for dogs must include thyroid replacement. This keeps the metabolic rate on track and enables the system to efficiently process foreign material—allergens and medication alike. Without thyroid replacement there is the risk of slowly creating side effects from the cortisone, even at low dosage. I discuss this in more detail in Chapter Nine.

If your veterinarian uses this long-term approach for allergies you can expect a very successful outcome. If you stop the program down the line the allergies will return.

Viruses, Bacteria, and Fungi

Repeated infections in dogs are often signs of endocrine-immune malfunction. It is not that animals never developed infections before, it is just that now they have more infections that are more difficult to treat.

Colds and flu

I treat many dogs who develop infections that we tend to associate more with people than animals. Often dogs will get sick a week or so after the owners have a cold or flu. There may be nasal involvement like a cold, a viral inflammation of the white of the eye, an upset gastrointestinal tract with vomiting and diarrhea, or an upper respiratory cough. If there are two dogs in the same household both may be affected. One might have a respiratory involvement and the other a digestive tract infection.

Many veterinarians do not recognize this as a flu-type syndrome. But that is what I see because the owners have been sick with the same thing.

Parvo

This viral condition, a close relative of feline distemper, is believed to have mutated from the cat and first infected dogs in the late 1970s. Parvovirus showed up first in Rottweilers and now is common in many breeds.

The virus primarily affects young dogs. It attacks the intestinal tract, permitting the entry of bacteria and toxins into the system and causing vomiting, diarrhea and fluid loss. Vaccinations are the main weapons used by veterinarians to protect puppies from parvo. Despite this, outbreaks still frequently occur. Many veterinarians believe this happens because the vaccine is not effective against different strains of parvo.

My experience suggests differently. I believe that vaccinated dogs who later develop parvo have endocrine-immune imbalances. The imbalances prevent the animals from producing the protective antibodies in response to the vaccination. I have heard that some dogs have been vaccinated every month up to eighteen months of age and still develop the infection. Such animals simply cannot make antibodies, and when they become exposed, they get the disease. The problem is not resistant, different strains. The problem is the imbalances.

Bacterial infections

Among the microorganisms residing in your dog's skin are staphylococcus bacteria that cause pyoderma. This is manifested as itchy skin that a dog scratches or chews at incessantly. Surface pyodermas are red, irritated, and often develop into raised, round scabs. Deeper involvement can produce abscesses with oozing, inflamed pustules.

Fleas, food allergies, and a compromised immune system often set the stage for pyoderma outbreaks. The endocrine-immune defect often lurks in the background. If the defect is severe, abscesses may develop throughout the skin and even internally, affecting the liver, kidney, pancreas, and other organs.

A dog with pyoderma is usually treated with antibiotics. The animal may improve for a while but frequently the problem returns because the immune system cannot mount an adequate defense in the face of multiple hormonal disturbances. Once the imbalances are identified and corrected, a restored immune system can keep the bacteria under control. Most healthy dogs have large colonies of staph living in their skin without any problem.

One particularly interesting case I treated involved a Golden Retriever. I tested the animal and started a hormone replacement program. However, the dog's owner was persuaded by his brother, a health professional, that the cortisone treatment could be dangerous. So he discontinued the therapy.

In the ensuing years, as I later learned, the young daughter of the dog's owner developed chronic staphylococcus pustules on her face. The father took the girl to pediatrician after pediatrician without resolving the problem. Finally, the seventh pediatrician learned that a dog lived in the house and suggested that the girl's condition might be related to exposure to the dog.

The father returned to my clinic with the dog. It had been five years since I first treated the animal. I repeated the endocrine-immune test and once again found the same imbalances. I also did a bacterial culture sensitivity test. The results turned up the same bacterial strain that had been found in the daughter's facial pustules. I started the dog on the same therapy program that had been discontinued years earlier. The condition cleared up. Interestingly, the client called me within a few weeks and excitedly reported that his daughter's condition had cleared up too without any new treatment whatsoever. The problem had been the girl's exposure to the infected dog. "I believe in your therapy now," the client said. "Nothing else was helping my dog or my daughter."

Young children have immature immune systems. They can develop a staph infection of their own—known as impetigo—when exposed to infected animals. Once the source is eliminated, the child is better able to respond to treatment and combat the infection.

Fungal infections

Veterinarians used to see a lot of fungal infections in Irish Setters and Bulldogs. However, these infections have spread across the breed landscape, chronically affecting ears and feet, or attacking internal tissue. One common cause is a compromised immune system too weak to overcome the fungi.

In the Southwest, a fungus called coccidioidomycosis has created considerable concern. This microorganism resides in the soil. When it becomes wind-borne people and animals inhale it, and an infectious process starts in the lungs called "valley fever." The infection can spread throughout the body and be fatal. Veterinarians treat valley fever with very expensive and potentially dangerous anti-fungal medications. Correcting the endocrine-immune defect is much safer—and effective.

Malabsorption and Digestive Tract Disorders

Malabsorption refers to an inability to properly absorb food through the intestinal lining for subsequent use in the body. If it continues long enough, malabsorption leads to nutrient deprivation, and if not remedied, leads to death. In animals, signs of an absorption problem include dandruff, hair loss, muscle weakness, and wasting.

When such signs appear, veterinarians may recommend feeding more or changing the diet. If these efforts fail, X-rays of the gut may be recommended to see if intestinal tumors or any other disturbances are interfering with absorption. When veterinarians find some roughness in the small intestine lining, they diagnose inflammatory bowel disease, and ulcerative colitis if the problem is located in the large intestine (colon). Nowadays, a good deal of inflammatory bowel disease is being diagnosed among all breeds.

Veterinarians may recommend a biopsy of affected gut tissue. On examination, they usually find the tissue brimming with immune cells such as plasma cells, eosinophils, and lymphocytes. Such excess indicates a disorder in progress that has major immune system involvement causing inflammation and swelling. To counteract the inflammation, practitioners will likely prescribe a cortisone medication.

Not recognized or looked for in this conventional scenario is an underlying deficiency of cortisol, the body's own natural anti-inflammatory. This deficiency, and the cascade of endocrine-immune chaos it generates, often leads to the inflammation and malabsorption. Estrogen is high. Thyroid hormones are bound. IgA antibodies that normally operate in the mucus membranes of the gut and protect this vital turf are operating abnormally without control, and even attack host tissue.

In this chaos, an effective defense is missing. Harmful bacteria and other microorganisms gain the upper hand, not only in the intestinal tract but often elsewhere in the body as well. The walls of the gut become inflamed and thicken, disturbing the normal uptake of nutrients from food breakdown.

What about absorption of medication prescribed for inflammatory bowel conditions? In the presence of inflammation and malabsorption, the oral cortisone probably will not work—or will not work well—because it, too, cannot be absorbed through the intestinal lining. When there is malabsorption oral medications tend to go in one end and out the other.

It is the same with antibiotics—they provide little help for malabsorption. Moreover, antibiotics may make matters worse because not only do they kill harmful bacteria in the gut but they also kill the beneficial bacteria that colonize the gut and form a major part of the body's defense system. This permits subsequent proliferation of harmful yeast organisms. Since 1972, I have consistently resolved these types of problems using endocrine-immune therapy.

If there is considerable inflammation and malabsorption, I start the therapeutic process with an intramuscular injection of cortisone that remains in the system for several weeks. This technique bypasses the challenge of absorption through the gut and quickly begins to remedy the cortisol deficiency. The estrogen level drops, IgA efficiency improves, and at a certain point when inflammation has decreased sufficiently in the intestinal tract, the animal can be switched to oral medication. As the chaos in the gut diminishes, the animal is also more able to absorb food. (I describe the injection protocol in detail in Chapter Nine.)

Digestive disorders often have an enzyme deficiency component as well. By that I mean the body does not produce enough good digestive enzymes to break down the highly processed commercial pet food that dogs typically eat. Frequently, this problem can be resolved simply with a healthy diet and a pet digestive enzyme supplement. (See Chapter Eleven on the enzyme issue.)

Autoimmune Diseases

At the core of a healthy immune response is the ability of immune cells to distinguish between "self" and "non-self." A natural intelligence regulates the system and guides the cells to correct targets such as harmful bacteria, viruses, or other pathogens. Regulated immune cells do not attack the body's own tissues—the "self." The trillions of cells that make up the different systems and organs within the body bear distinctive molecules. These molecules are like chemical name tags that identify the cells as part of the "self" and these are not attacked as alien material by the immune system.

When orderliness is lost, for whatever reason, the immune system may start to attack the "self." Medicine calls this an autoimmune disease. In humans, lupus and rheumatoid arthritis are well-known autoimmune conditions. Dogs also develop autoimmune diseases. The most common is discoid lupus, recognized by a butterfly-shaped lesion on the nose. The dog will scratch a good deal and be regarded as a "poor doer." As the condition worsens, anemia and pustules develop, and the dog can die.

In autoimmune hemolytic anemia, the body attacks its own red blood cells. This, too, can be fatal. Pemphigus, another autoimmune condition, involves the immune system attacking the muco-cutaneous junction, which is where the skin joins mucous tissue. You may see red, inflamed tissue in the eyelids, and around the mouth and rectum. Scabs, and sometimes bleeding, will develop. This, too, can be deadly if not corrected.

Dogs also develop rheumatoid arthritis, a painful and debilitating autoimmune condition of the joints. Here the body attacks healthy joint tissue, causing inflammation and subsequent damage. The joints of the elbows, ankles, and wrists swell, and feel warm to the touch. Over time, the animal may become lame.

I have helped numerous animals with these types of problems by correcting the endocrine-immune imbalances. The therapy restores regulation back to a de-regulated immune system. When imbalances exist, regulation is lacking, and immune cells lose their guiding intelligence and ability to discriminate between "self" and "non-self." Without control, they lash out at both.

In the early years of my practice I did not treat many cases of autoimmune disease. But as the genetic defect has spread, so has the incidence of disease. The progression has been faster in some breeds, slower in others. In the beginning I usually saw these problems in older animals but now I see them routinely in young dogs who are only two, three, or even younger.

I often find the endocrine-immune problem in the mother and/or the father of affected puppies. With subsequent generations the imbalance tends to become more profound. Parents may have had minimum imbalance that did not cause clinical problems. But when they mate, multiple littermates are hit with the defect. Some of the offspring may suffer outright, while others carry the defect onward to the next generation. Breeders often tell me they never saw this before. Now they are desperate for help.

Cancer

According to the American Veterinary Medical Association, dogs develop cancer at about the same rate as humans. The incidence increases with age, and accounts for almost half of canine deaths over the age of ten years. Many veterinarians are concerned, however, about a sharp rise in cancer among much younger animals. This has certainly been my observation as well. I see cancer among dogs as young as one, two, and three years of age. I never saw that when I started in my veterinary practice in 1966.

In a recent book, *The Veterinarians' Guide to Natural Remedies for Dogs* (Three Rivers Press, 2000), my co-author Martin Zucker interviewed three dozen practitioners who specialize in alternative veterinary medicine. It was their consensus that "the incidence of cancer…is a failure of the immune system in the face of genetic weaknesses fostered by contemporary breeding practices and a constant onslaught of poor diet, medication, toxic chemicals, vaccines, and stress."

I certainly subscribe to that general assessment, and will go one step further. When I test cancer patients for endocrine-immune imbalances, they turn up in each and every case. Every animal has them! Hormonal imbalances starting in the adrenal gland with cortisol set off a harmful sequence of internal disturbances in the body. The falling dominos reach the immune system, and it too falls, and fails to contain abnormally mutating weak cancer cells from growing rapidly. A compromised defense means the dog has no weapons with which to fight back. In one animal the disease may develop as a skin tumor such as squamous cell in the jaw or mouth. In another, breast cancer, lymphoma, fibrous sarcoma, or leukemia. The impact area varies from animal to animal but these are the same cancers that physicians see in people.

I have corrected imbalances in very young dogs from canine families in which cancer has already killed littermates. These "corrected" animals have gone on to live long lives. Some have developed cancer at eleven, twelve, or thirteen years of age, or some not at all. Often I have been able to provide help to patients who were considered terminal. Even in these advanced cases, the endocrine-immune program has frequently worked to extend the lives of otherwise doomed animals.

If veterinarians can remedy the endocrine-immune defect and restore the impaired processes as much as possible, they may be able to wholly prevent the cancer in genetically predisposed animals. If not complete prevention, they may at least keep the disease in check for many years, or keep terminally ill animals alive longer and with a better quality of life.

Obviously, the prospects for defeating cancer or any other type of serious disease are always better if the condition has not advanced and already created major damage. If surgery, radiation, and chemotherapy are indicated, as they often are, the hormone replacement therapy can be extremely supportive, and, in fact, may even ensure the success of those treatments. Conventional methods may not stop the cancer from recurring, but in conjunction with the hormonal therapy there may be total containment. Whether early or advanced cancer, the patient acquires a powerful self-healing tool by repairing the endocrine-immune mechanism. Without this basic repair work, the healing may not take place.

I strongly believe that scientific research into the cortisol connection could yield a wealth of information that may benefit the prevention and treatment of cancer. As a clinician, I do not have the resources for that kind of research. My clinical experience in testing and treating these animals has been very gratifying. I cannot say that I "cure" cancer with this approach, but many of the animals I treat go on to have long and healthy lives.

Kidney Disease

Kidneys remove waste products from the blood. It is a critical job. In an age of poor-quality pet food and constant exposure to toxic chemicals, the task is even more critical and burdensome. No wonder that kidney disease affects a great number of dogs, many of whom suffer from a progressive loss of filtering capacity as they get older. Inside the kidneys, inflammation and scar tissue develop and interfere with normal function. If the kidneys do not effectively eliminate wastes, a potentially fatal buildup of internal poisons called uremia can occur.

Signs of decreased kidney function include excessive thirst, vomiting, weight loss, poor appetite, poor coat, heavy shedding, and the smell of urine on the skin. Another good indicator is urination that produces only a small amount of urine.

Veterinarians used to see a high rate of this among Miniature Schnauzers. Now we see kidney disease in all breeds, and at a much younger age. It is no longer an old-age problem. We see many young dogs, animals even just a year old, with terminal kidneys. Something has damaged the functional units in those young organs.

The unrecognized cause, once again, is often the endocrine-immune defect. In the kidneys it creates considerable inflammation that chokes off the normal filtering activity. Just as in the digestive tract, deregulated immune cells can no longer protect the mucous linings inside the organ. The result is an autoimmune-like reaction and bacterial proliferation. A urinary tract antibiotic such as Baytril may provide only partial relief, because it does not address the underlying problem.

A veterinarian will often prescribe a low-protein diet. The idea is to ease the burden on the weakened kidneys struggling to remove the waste products from protein breakdown. I believe this approach is flawed. The protein may be lower in volume, but it is usually bad protein, full of impurities that the body has to process out.

Chronic Liver Disease

This used to be an old dog's disease, part of the slowing-down process. Signs are low energy, a decreased appetite, and perhaps vomiting, irritability, and jaundice. The stool may look yellowish.

Now veterinarians see chronic liver disease in young animals, even at one or two years of age. Veterinarians are not sure why this is happening in animals so young. My theory is that the endocrine-immune defect is involved. The defect's characteristic combination of low cortisol and elevated estrogen impairs the thyroid hormones, the substances that govern the metabolic rate of the body. With less thyroid hormones available, the body runs slower.

The liver is the central detoxification organ of the body. Endocrine-immune imbalances may cause it to run in slow motion, so to speak. Toxins, preservatives, and bodily waste products stay in the liver longer where they can damage the liver cells. Poison builds up. Scar tissue forms. It is a situation akin to cirrhosis of the liver, but without the alcohol. Here, it is a hormonally induced poisoning of the liver. The liver is being slowly destroyed, and eventually, the buildup of poison kills the animal.

Von Willebrand's Disease

This bleeding disorder was first seen in Doberman Pinschers. Now it has spread to many breeds. Basically, there exists a hemophiliac effect, which is a problem with blood clotting. A simple cut bleeds and bleeds. Spaying an affected dog can result in an alarming quantity of blood.

Again, I believe the underlying mechanism is the same low cortisol and high estrogen situation. The combination impairs thyroid hormones, which slows down the body's metabolic processes. The clotting factor is negatively affected as a part of this slowdown.

Veterinarians are unable to treat this disease effectively. They may use vitamin K, clotting medication, and even transfusions, but these treatments only help temporarily. In my opinion, the disease is a secondary effect—the result of bound or deficient thyroid and an adrenal defect.

Behavioral Problems

Emotional stability often suffers when hormones are out of sync. Animals may develop aggressiveness, anxiety, or fear, and even run away. Such problems often cause an owner to give up on a pet. I have traced many of these emotion-related issues to hormonal imbalances. Once I correct the imbalances the problem vanishes.

Aggression

Unpredictable aggression or "rage syndrome" now commonly occurs in all breeds and in one form or another. Dogs suddenly attack other animals or people, or both, and even their owners.

This is an issue that goes beyond a dog defending his or her territory or asserting dominance over other animals. It is not a matter of a sentry dog guarding a warehouse and attacking a trespasser. That dog has been designed for a certain function and trained a certain way. I am referring to common household pets and unprovoked, unexpected attacks. The kids may be playing around the dog and all of a sudden the dog gets a funny look in his eyes, and you are not sure whether he is going to attack or not.

Where did this come from? If you talk to people in rescue organizations they often say, "The poor dog was abused." Well, an abused dog should know who did the abusing. A dog should also know who is doing the loving and recognize friendly family members.

Rescue people are hard pressed to explain such aggressive behavior. Often they turn to the training option. "We'll train the bad behavior out of the dog," they say. Training, of course, can play a role. But if the dog is not trained correctly and has hormonal imbalances to begin with, the aggressiveness could become worse. Frequently I find a hormonal imbalance problem as a backdrop to aggressiveness.

The cortisol defect induces a rise in testosterone and estrogen from the adrenal glands in both male and female animals. Too much testosterone is associated with aggression. In research with humans, elevated estrogen has been suggested as a significant factor causing aggressive behavior in both sexes. When I correct the imbalances in aggressive patients, the aggression subsides in virtually all of them. This is true whether they are spayed, neutered, or intact.

I have heard many reports of behavioral problems among breeds such as Cocker and Springer Spaniels who have been bred for certain looks instead of for their traditional hunting and field functions. I recall the case of a Springer who was a show animal. The owner said the dog was attacking the judges at dog shows. I did a workup and found a cortisol imbalance with elevated estrogen. After initiating an appropriate hormone replacement program, along with a special diet, the hostile behavior was eliminated and the dog could be shown again.

Hypersexuality in neutered or spayed animals

A spayed or neutered dog mounting another dog is not an uncommon sight. Hormonal imbalances, starting with a deficiency of cortisol, can trigger this behavior. An excess of estrogen and testosterone may develop and promote residual sexuality even though the animal has been spayed or neutered.

Separation anxiety

In early 1999, the U.S. Food and Drug Administration announced approval of the first "antidepressant" drug for dogs. "Clomicalm" was designed for canines suffering from separation anxiety, which is an emotional crisis triggered when owners leave the house. For some anxious dogs, such abandonment can unleash prolonged barking episodes, gnawing on a leg or other body part, or destructive behavior in the house.

Nicholas Dodman, B.V.M.S., of the Tufts University School of Veterinary Medicine, says as many as 10 percent of dogs may have this problem and "it is serious in 40 percent of these," according to a 1999 report in the *Los Angeles Times.*

I have treated animals who jumped through glass windows because of their anxiety. One young Mastiff I treated practically ate his owner's couch and then chewed the door down. These animals respond very well to replacement hormones. The endocrine-immune program reduces elevated estrogen that may be causing inflammation in arterial tissue leading to the brain, effects that could possibly trigger behavioral problems.

Epilepsy

Epileptic seizures are fairly common in dogs. An affected animal may experience a *petit mal,* a minor seizure often characterized by spasms in a leg or one or more groups of muscles. A more severe *grand mal* episode can last from a few seconds to many minutes, and may involve loss of consciousness, a more generalized spasm, and possibly jerking, salivating, and uncontrolled urination. A dog may appear confused and exhausted afterward.

Epilepsy is a complex issue without simple answers. Genetics, toxic exposures, allergies, and trauma may all have a role in creating a "short" in the wiring of the nervous system. However, medical science does not have all the answers yet as to how epilepsy happens. The conventional response is to administer central nervous depressants—such as phenobarbital—for the remainder of a patient's life.

In the 1970s, veterinarians saw many seizure problems among Poodles. The breed had become very popular. Breeders wanted to sell and a lot of people wanted to buy. So cosmetic inbreeding became widespread for the "Poodle look," and with this trend came the genetic problems. Today, however, veterinarians see epilepsy across the board in other breeds and in entire litters.

In my experience, all dogs who suffer from so-called idiopathic epileptic seizures, that is, where the cause is not understood, have underlying food sensitivities The problem goes right back to endocrine-immune imbalances. With the loss of proper hormonal regulation of the immune system, a certain food or a fleabite may set off an allergic reaction in a susceptible animal that can generate uncontrolled electrical activity in the brain and manifest as a convulsion.

It is interesting to note that many animals who take anti-epileptic prescriptions such as phenobarbital absorb medication poorly because of inflammation in the gut related to a deficiency of IgA antibodies. The intestinal turmoil may block out a lot of the medication and thus not prevent seizures from occurring.

Obesity

Obesity is the number one nutritional disorder among dogs. Studies suggest that about one-quarter of all dogs treated at veterinary clinics are overweight. Just like humans, the added weight increases the risk of cardiovascular, respiratory, and skeletal system problems.

Certain breeds are said to be more susceptible to obesity than others. They include Beagles, Basset Hounds, Dachshunds, and Labrador Retrievers, however, I see fat dogs among all breeds. The overweight problem is generally attributed to excess calories in the food, too little exercise, a genetic predisposition, and hormonal disorders. Hormone imbalances, for instance, may result from castration and spaying, resulting in reduced activity and changes in metabolism. Dysfunction of the thyroid or pituitary glands can also lead to weight problems.

In my practice, I have linked many cases of obesity to endocrine-immune imbalances that interfere with the thyroid hormones. A blood test for thyroid function may show the hormones in the normal range, however, if the hormones are bound, a normal score does not mean anything. There is still not enough active hormone to do the job. As a result, the whole metabolism slows down and more calories become stored instead of burned.

The key is to check the estrogen level. If high, it is binding thyroid. Once you correct that with the therapy I recommend in Chapter Nine, you can restore your heavyweight dog back to his or her natural weight level.

An additional cause of weight gain in animals is a digestive enzyme deficiency, a problem I address in Chapter Eleven.

− FIVE −

Imbalanced Cats

The adrenal defect—unseen, unrecognized, and undiagnosed by most veterinarians—lurks behind many of the major health problems that afflict cats: urinary tract disorders, cancer, and the devastating retroviral diseases. The defect continues to impair resistance and vitality, leaving cats more vulnerable to infections and allergies. The unsuspected imbalances destroy critical defense mechanisms in intestinal tissue, promoting the development of inflammatory bowel disease.

In dogs, my experience has been that the imbalances undermine normal thyroid function. As a result, about 90 percent of the canine cases I treat require thyroid replacement in addition to low dosage cortisone. In cats, thyroid is much less of an issue. Only about 10 percent of sick, endocrine-immune defective cats need thyroid. These are animals who are genuinely hypothyroid (low thyroid) cats or who have feline infectious peritonitis (FIP), and they require both cortisone and thyroid replacement for resolution. I discuss this point in the FIP section in this chapter.

Allergies

The same principle applies for cats as discussed in Chapter Four on allergies in dogs. Today's cats, like dogs, are developing surface signs of allergies at younger ages. Typical indicators are persistent biting, licking, or scratching of skin; inflamed skin, lumps, bumps, or recurring sores; and inflamed ears with repeated infections.

Flea bites, over-vaccination, and the proliferation of chemicals are commonly cited as triggers for allergic conditions. Add one more to the list: the endocrine-immune defect. It is a major cause. By correcting it, pets are protected against allergies, including miliary dermatitis, a frequent affliction characterized by small bumps, sores, and scabs around the head, neck, and back. Cats with this condition are miserable and may lose their appetite. They will typically take a step or two, then stop and scratch. Often, they will tear, lick, or chew out parcels of hair. As a result, they frequently develop hair balls.

Viruses, Bacteria, and Fungi
Viral infections

Long ago, conventional medicine adopted the germ theory of Louis Pasteur and designed its treatments to destroy germs. Later in his career Pasteur saw a major flaw in his theory. He declared that germs do not cause disease unless the organism is in a weakened state. "The germ is nothing," he said, "the terrain is everything."

The terrain is the body's immune system. The question is whether it is strong or weak. If a cat has a weak system and bumps into another cat who is infected or has a disease, the first cat may quickly develop the same disease. Viruses can also infiltrate the cat, lie dormant for a period of time, even years, then replicate and attack, causing serious damage and even death. Cat-specific viral infections include:

- FeLV (feline leukemia)
- FIP (feline infectious peritonitis)
- FIV (feline immunosuppressive virus)

From my perspective, the ability of cats to fight off viruses such as these hinges on their endocrine-immune resources. The hormonal defect typically compromises the ability of animals to put up a good defense. Immune cells are deregulated and suppressed. When a cat dies, people say the virus killed the animal. In my opinion it is more a case of a dysfunctional immune system that has not only failed to deter a virus challenge but which has also turned on the cat and helped to kill the animal.

If the defect is present, do not expect much protection from vaccinations. The cat may not respond to immunizations by producing the necessary antibodies to ward off the viruses. I find many animals vulnerable—and at serious risk—to viruses and other microorganisms because of the unsuspected lack of antibody production following vaccinations. If a cat gets the disease after being vaccinated veterinarians will often suspect a "different feline leukemia." It is not a different leukemia. The vaccine just has not done its job because a dysfunctional immune system could not respond appropriately. The patient could not make antibodies to the vaccine or mount a vigorous immune response when exposed.

It is thought that these viruses can readily spread from one infected cat to other felines in the household. In my experience, this is true only if the other cats have the endocrine-immune defect. Without the defect, cats usually can mount an effective defense. Thus, if one cat in a multi-cat house comes down with a serious case of FeLV, FIP, or FIV, I strongly recommend having the other cats tested for the defect. (See Chapter Eight.) If they have the defect, consider doing the cortisol replacement therapy described in Chapter Nine. That will protect them. If the test shows no defect, do not worry, just monitor the situation. For symptomatic cats who are generally considered incurable, the hormone replacement program could be helpful. The therapy has a high rate of success when done correctly.

If a cat does not have clinical signs of illness, but is nevertheless positive for any of these viruses, I highly recommend that you ask your veterinarian to do the endocrine-immune test. If the results indicate no imbalance, it is highly unlikely the animal will get the disease. If the results indicate imbalance, correct it before the cat becomes sick.

After starting on the hormone replacement program a cat often will test negative for the virus. This is true whether the cat previously tested positive or actually showed clinical signs of disease. The underlying defect has been corrected. The immune cells are effectively fighting and destroying the viruses.

This has been my experience in numerous cases, including large catteries. Multiple felines under one roof might test positive for a particular virus but the huge majority of them live long and healthy lives if they are put back into hormonal balance.

Your veterinarian can test for the defect. If present, you and your veterinarian can work together to correct it. The therapy puts a cat's derailed immune system back on track, enabling him or her to fight off any virus. The cat will test negative. I have seen this reversal so many times that it does not surprise me anymore, even though the veterinary textbooks say it does not happen. Supposedly once a cat has the virus, he or she always has it. But that is not my clinical experience.

Veterinarians frequently use chemotherapy to treat these conditions. Chemo is designed to suppress the immune system. But what if the immune system is already damaged and suppressed? And what if the endocrine system is also damaged and out of balance? The danger is that chemo will further damage both systems and contribute to the death of the patient.

The adrenal defect, if it exists, needs to be corrected—the earlier the better, before organs and vital parts sustain severe damage. The defect produces elevated estrogen. If the level is high enough it can suppress bone marrow and red blood cell production. The cat will develop anemia, and blood transfusions may be needed.

Examination and laboratory tests are necessary to determine a precise diagnosis for these major viral diseases. Clinical signs can be confusing and often overlap with other conditions.

Feline Leukemia Virus (FeLV)

The leukemia virus can strike almost any tissue or organ and open the door for a variety of associated diseases. An animal may develop anemia, diarrhea or constipation, enlarged lymph nodes, loss of energy and appetite, and infertility. Some infected cats also develop malignant masses and a dangerous lymph-related cancer called lymphosarcoma. Physical damage takes place depending on where the virus concentrates and where there may be areas of genetic weakness.

On hormone replacement, I have been able to save about 85 percent of these leukemic animals. Those who do not survive have usually suffered too much physical damage already from the disease process. They are beyond the point of repair and cannot respond to the therapy.

Other veterinarians who use my approach report a similar high level of success. One such veterinarian contacted me to describe how he successfully treated a cat who previously had been under treatment for two months at a university clinic. The university vets basically gave up on the cat. The veterinarian who used my method healed the cat.

Feline Infectious Peritonitis (FIP)

Cats become infected with FIP through direct contact with sick felines or by contact with virus-contaminated surfaces such as clothing, feeding bowls, or bedding. The virus is shed through the saliva and feces. Exposure may cause a temporary and mild upper respiratory illness with sneezing, watery eyes, and nasal discharge. Most cats completely recover from that. A small percentage, however, develop the clinical signs of deadly FIP weeks, months, or even longer after their primary infection.

FIP comes in different forms: wet, dry, or a combination of both. In the wet form, the abdomen and/or chest fill with fluid, making it difficult for the cat to breathe. Fever, anemia, depression, and weight loss characterize the dry form.

All the FIP cats I test have the adrenal defect and deregulated immune systems that cannot distinguish between the virus and the host. So the immune system attacks the body as well as the virus.

In the standard treatment for FIP, malabsorption is routinely overlooked. The cat's gut is inflamed. It cannot really absorb much—food or medication—and antibiotics often have little effect for this reason.

The treatment protocol I have developed starts with testing for the endocrine-immune imbalance. If the imbalance is found, the replacement therapy for this condition requires two things: cortisone and thyroid. For some unknown reason, FIP affects the thyroid. Other than FIP and a clear case of hypothyroidism, I have not found it necessary to prescribe thyroid for cats.

For the first week or two, medication such as cortisone and antibiotics, along with nutrients, are administered on an IV or intramuscular basis to circumvent a likely malabsorption situation in the gut. Once immunity improves and the malabsorption corrected, oral medications work fine.

Thyroid can be given orally. It appears to be absorbed adequately because the molecular size of the medication is small enough to penetrate even an inflamed gut.

The antibiotics are involved for the short term, the cortisone and thyroid for the long term. Using this approach I have been able to save about 70 percent of the sick FIP cats I treat.

Feline Immunodeficiency Virus (FIV)

FIV, a relatively new viral villain on the feline health scene, is the equivalent of the HIV virus in humans. Researchers say it does not spread to humans. It is species specific. Over time it reduces the immune system's ability to combat other viruses and microorganisms, leaving an animal highly vulnerable to secondary, fatal infections. The virus primarily spreads through bite wounds. Outdoor male cats are most commonly affected.

FIV causes a generalized enlargement of the lymph nodes. Signs of active infection include poor coat, persistent fever, loss of appetite, weight loss and wasting away, anemia, and inflammation of the gums, mouth, skin, bladder, and upper respiratory tract. Most of the time cats with clear signs of disease are euthanized.

I recommend to clients that we test for the endocrine-immune imbalance. If imbalance is present, the animal needs cortisol replacement for a lifetime. As in other viral conditions, the veterinarian should be alert for intestinal inflammation. Such inflammation can block the absorption of oral medication or hormone replacement.

Proper, long-term replacement therapy can help 70 percent of cats with active infections live long and healthy lives. Moreover, these once extremely sick cats often shed the virus.

Feline acne

Cats with acne display blackhead-like growths full of bloody pus that may rupture. Tissue swells up and mimics a cat bite abscess or a tooth root infection. You may see skin eruptions and pustules. This common condition may be localized to the jaw area and chin, or spread to other surface areas of the body. The greater the endocrine-immune imbalance in the system, the more likely it will spread. It is a case of insufficient resistance, which permits bacteria to essentially "eat" the body.

Fungal infections

Simple exposure to fungus can cause ringworm, a condition in kittens associated with round areas of hair loss with raised, red pigmentation. Internal fungus infections can cause epilepsy, impaired respiration, staggering, and lack of intestinal motility. My clinical experience indicates that the endocrine-immune imbalance lowers resistance and allows for the spread of yeast, cryptococcosis, hystoplasmosis, and other fungal microorganisms.

Malabsorption and Digestive Disorders

Intestinal disorders and malabsorption have become huge problems among cats. Things have gotten so bad that inflammatory bowel disease support groups have formed around the country.

Trouble signs are chronic vomiting, diarrhea, and weight loss. See a veterinarian if they develop. Resultant dehydration can be life threatening.

Veterinary researchers do not know the exact cause of inflammatory bowel disease but their reports indicate the presence of a good deal of abnormal B and T immune cell activity in the gut. As I explained in the previous chapter, I believe much of this disorder relates to a deficiency of IgA antibody, a primary immune defender in the mucous linings of the body.

Standard procedure involves the use of oral cortisone medication to reduce the inflammation. However, the oral medications usually do not work well because the patient can not absorb them. The turmoil rages on, and the animal gradually wastes away. Conventional treatment also focuses on variations of specialized diets to eliminate food sensitivities. If these approaches are not successful, veterinarians often apply powerful immunosuppressive drugs. In my opinion, such potent drugs only serve to further weaken and destabilize a dysfunctional immune system.

Affected animals usually have a similar underlying endocrine-immune problem. That is why cortisone therapy is effective. It corrects the initiating defect in these disorders—a cortisol deficiency. But the therapy needs to be continued on a low-dosage basis; otherwise the intestinal chaos will likely return.

Cancer

As with dogs, veterinarians are treating more cases of cancer in cats than ever before. When I started out in practice I treated cancer mostly among Siamese, Burmese, and Abyssinians. But now the disease is much more widespread, becoming an equal opportunity killer.

I test for the endocrine-immune imbalance in all my cancer cases, and I find it in every case—without exception. Each and every cancer patient has it. The imbalance is primary, the cancer a secondary effect. By fixing the primary hormonal problem the odds are significantly changed to beat the cancer.

Urinary Tract Disorders

At least 10 percent of cats suffer chronically with feline urinary syndrome (FUS), also known as feline lower urinary tract disease

(FLUTD). The names of the disease may be different but the problem is the same—trouble in the kidneys, bladder, and/or the urethra, the narrow tube that carries urine out of the body.

The disorder has two aspects:
1) Infections, generally caused by bacterial, fungal, or parasitic agents.
2) "Stones," comprised of minerals, mucous, cellular debris and other material in the bladder or urethra. This problem is more dangerous for male cats because the particles can partially or wholly plug up the urethra, which is narrower and longer in males than in females. Any such obstruction can shut down the kidneys and cause a life-threatening emergency. A bladder can rupture, or a cat can become poisoned from a backup of urine and die within one or two days.

Signs are usually similar and quite dramatic—a cat straining and making repeated, prolonged attempts to pass urine. Sometimes only a few drops will pass through. An affected cat may be in a great deal of pain. Do not waste time. See a veterinarian as fast as possible. Other signs of urinary tract trouble may include:

- Licking the genital area excessively
- Urinating outside the litter box
- Spending a lot of time in the litter box
- Blood in the urine
- Lethargy
- Poor appetite
- Breath smells of urine

Over the years, veterinary researchers have put forward a number of theories as to why stones form. First, they incriminated a diet high in ash, which is the mineral content of food. Pet food manufacturers responded and produced low-ash diets. That did not solve the problem. In the mid-1980s, researchers put the blame on magnesium. Specifically, they found that magnesium oxide, an alkaline compound, promoted stones when added to the food, but magnesium chloride, an acidic compound, dissolved crystals. The problem, it seemed, was not ash, and not really magnesium, but the pH of the urine. Acidic conditions discouraged crystal buildup.

Alkaline encouraged crystals. This finding gave rise to acid-producing foods.

But results were mixed. Typical urinary tract stones are made up of either magnesium ammonium phosphate (also known as struvite) or calcium oxalate. The higher acidic diets reduced the incidence of the alkaline struvite stones. However, there has been a disturbing rise in calcium oxalate stones as a result of strongly acidic urine. So at the present the diet connection remains murky, with no evidence that special diets bring down the incidence of urinary tract disease.

Despite extensive diagnostic tests, researchers are unsure about the causes of more than half the cases. They describe such situations as idiopathic feline lower urinary tract disease (IFLUTD). Idiopathic refers to a condition that arises from an unknown or obscure cause.

Sometimes with chronic problems in male cats, veterinarians will perform urethrostomies. They cut about three-quarters of an inch off the penis at the point where the urethra inside is narrowest and plugs up. So the male now has a shorter penis, but wider urethra. Any new stones that come along should pass right out as with female cats. This procedure, of course, does not address the cause. A cat with an amputated penis still develops stones.

There can be a multiplicity of reasons why felines develop urinary tract disorders. I have had great success preventing and treating this problem by correcting the endocrine-immune defect. Here is how I believe the defect affects the urinary tract:

1) The cat is born with, or acquires, a cortisol defect.
2) The resultant loss of immune regulation impacts different systems in different animals. It commonly causes dysfunctional or suppressed IgA activity in both the digestive and urinary tracts. Keep in mind that IgA is the paramount antibody involved in protecting mucous tissues. An IgA deficiency can lead to inflammation, irritation, and poor resistance in the mucous linings of both systems.
3) In the digestive tract, some degree of inflammation develops. The inflammation may be subclinical—low grade—but it is significant enough to cause some degree of malabsorption. Digestive processes work less efficiently. Proteins are harder to

break down and are not well absorbed. Carbohydrates are more easily broken down. The abundance of sugars—the breakdown product of carbohydrates—causes an alkaline pH to develop in the bloodstream and urine. This contributes to struvite stone formation. Moreover, an alkaline environment may promote bacterial growth that, aside from IgA involvement, can create inflammation.

4) One of the common blockage problems relates to a buildup of a toothpaste-like material that obstructs the urethra, primarily in males. The pasty substance develops out of excess mucous produced by the juxtaglomerular cells in the kidneys. This material subsequently mixes with grit and cellular debris picked up in the urinary tract. The overproduction of mucous may be due to the irritating histamine-like effect of a high estrogen level, one of the signature elements of the endocrine-immune imbalance.

5) Why does one cat block up from outright stones and another from the development of the pasty buildup? The reason is not clear. It may simply have to do with the genetic and biochemical differences. The point is that either of these situations can develop.

My treatment strategy is to first normalize endocrine-immune values if they are out of sync. Results are usually excellent. Once done, most cats can usually eat what they want without problems. Once corrected, I suggest that veterinarians check the urine pH. If it is still on the alkaline side, add more good protein to the diet. If it is on the acidic side, add carbohydrate. If pH normalization is still elusive, you may want to add a plant-based digestive enzyme supplement to the diet. This will promote a more effective breakdown of all nutrients—protein, carbohydrate, and fat. Refer to Chapter Eleven for details on enzyme supplements. About 20 percent of the time, a male cat will continue to plug after the endocrine-immune imbalance has been corrected. If this happens twice I suggest that the cat undergo a urethrostomy.

Chronic Liver Disease

Degeneration of the liver has long been considered an "old cat problem," but nowadays veterinarians see it in younger animals too. Liver problems produce trouble throughout the body. That is because this central organ masterminds the processing and utilization of nutrients as well as the removal of toxic substances. If you suspect a problem with the liver, be sure to obtain a professional diagnosis immediately. Signs of a failing liver can be easily confused with many different medical problems. Vomiting, lethargy, poor appetite, and jaundice are common indicators.

The endocrine-immune imbalance may contribute substantially to liver problems. Cortisol is deficient. Estrogen is high. Thyroid hormones become bound. This causes a slowdown throughout the system, including the liver's critical processing operations. If, for instance, the liver cannot detox properly, a buildup of wastes and toxins occurs. This aggravates the liver, and can cause a wide variety of trouble signs that point to liver disease. If the hormonal defect is involved, the liver disease is not a primary condition. It is secondary to the defect. The key to recovery is to correct the defect before severe liver damage has occurred.

Correction may also prevent heavy cats from developing life-threatening hepatic lipidosis—the so-called "fatty liver syndrome." Binding of thyroid hormone activity creates the equivalent of a hypothyroid condition—a situation where not enough thyroid hormone is available in the body. Hypothyroid patients are usually very heavy with excess fat in the body. Some of the fat becomes deposited in the liver, which congests the liver even more.

This same thyroid problem contributes to obesity. I have had people bring in twenty-five pound cats and say their animal hardly eats a thing. It does not matter. They can feed these animals nothing and they still may stay fat. Obesity is a secondary effect to the endocrine-immune mechanism.

Behavioral Problems

Aggression

The high estrogen level caused by the defect appears to bring out the tiger in many cats, both males and females. They may stalk their owners, then bite and scratch them.

Once, a new client showed me multiple scratch marks on her arms. "I tell people I got them working in my rose garden," she said. "Well, I do not have a rose garden. But I have a cat that has attacked me several times and become very unpredictable." I frequently hear stories like this. Fortunately, here is a behavioral problem that often responds well to hormone replacement therapy.

Unexpected spraying

On many occasions, clients have told me that their spayed females are spraying like a tom, or that their neutered males are still spraying. "I wonder if my cat was really fixed?" they'll ask.

Hormonal imbalances can explain both of these situations: spayed or neutered cats who are spraying. The pituitary secretes ACTH, the hormone that stimulates cortisol production from the middle layer of the adrenal cortex. However, if the cortisol defect exists, the middle layer cannot respond appropriately. The inner layer responds by releasing androgen hormones that can subsequently convert into testosterone. A rising concentration of male hormone could cause altered male or female cats to act like unneutered males. They spray walls and mark their territory.

There is a widely held belief that if you neuter males before one year of age, and supposedly remove the source of testosterone, they will never spray again. The problem with this concept is that the gonads are not the only source of testosterone. The testosterone can be adrenally induced as well.

Epilepsy

Seizures are not as common in cats as in dogs. However, just as in canines, an unsuspected and underlying cortisol defect can be involved. Frequently a problem with food sensitivities also exists. (See Chapter Six on environmental influences.)

Undiagnosed malabsorption may be present due to inflammation in the gut. Malabsorption often blocks uptake and utilization of medication. An affected animal may continue having seizures despite taking an anti-convulsive drug. For more details, refer to my comments about epilepsy in Chapter Four.

− SIX −

Environmental Influences:
Food, Fleas, and Toxins

Each and every body—mine, yours, your pet's—has a certain tolerance for handling the environmental inputs we are exposed to on a daily basis. Think of this tolerance as a barrel. Each of us has a barrel with a different capacity based on genetic inheritance. That is part of our individuality. Thus each of us can handle different degrees of stress. If you exceed your barrel's capacity it will spill over. Signs and symptoms of illness develop.

Why one individual—or animal—becomes affected at a certain time and not another can be explained by the individual differences of barrel capacity. Two Saint Bernards coming from the same litter will likely have two different capacities, as will two Persian cats from the same litter, or two brothers and sisters from the same human parents.

Stress can result from excessive physical activity, overwork, extreme cold or heat, infections, drugs, poor diet, food impurities, environmental and food chemicals, vaccinations, emotional disturbances, accidents, or surgery. The endocrine-immune defect effectively shrinks the barrel. It takes less input to cause an overflow and the appearance of distress or actual clinical signs of illness. Physical or emotional problems surface depending on weaknesses in the system. For one animal, the weakness may be located in the digestive tract; for another, the urinary tract or the nervous system; for another, all of the above. In my practice, I see many affected dogs and cats with multiple conditions. Often these animals are handicapped by defective adrenal glands that render them less able to cope with the stresses that life delivers. They react more and they suffer more.

A number of environmental influences—such as food, fleas, and toxins—typically act as stimuli that can overload the barrel. Whether you call them allergies, sensitivities, or whatever, I consider them to be largely secondary factors. A flawed endocrine-immune mechanism triggers a vicious cycle in which environmental factors participate in, and accelerate, a downward spiral of disease and premature death. This is why I treat the adrenal-immune defect first, and support it with a good solid diet. This approach effectively enhances the capacity of an animal's barrel so that environmental challenges no longer cause problems, or if they do, the problems are minimal.

Food

Food sustains life. But for many animals, that is not the case, as the following examples demonstrate.

- Billy was an orange tabby I treated years ago. From time to time he would develop thickened and inflamed ears. He would scratch at them so hard that he developed "cauliflower ears." Sometimes his ears bled from all the scratching. It turned out that Billy was highly sensitive to tuna. The cat's owner had a stepson who was very fond of the animal and whenever he visited he would bring fresh tuna. It was after the visits that the scratching started.
- Buck was a black Labrador who suffered constantly with lick granulomas. He would bite and chew on his legs and paws, creating inflammation and large, thickened strawberry-sized wounds. A previous veterinarian had tried all kinds of standard treatments on Buck without success. Ointments and medication stopped the persistent itchiness only temporarily. So Buck's legs were bandaged and an Elizabethan restraining collar put around his neck. When the bandages and collar came off after five weeks, the skin on his legs was much improved, but Buck immediately began the frenzied licking and chewing again. His legs were soon a bloody mess. At this point the dog was referred to me. I found out that he was eating a high potency kibble product containing multiple ingredients that I consider potentially problematic for many animals. They certainly were problematic for Buck.

Many years ago a breeder gave me a sweet Pomeranian puppy. I took the puppy home to share the household with my great Old

English Bulldog, Moose. Unfortunately, the Pomeranian took an instant dislike to Moose so I had to find a new home for the puppy. A friend took him in and gave him great care. The dog was leading a normal, uneventful life until one morning my friend's husband fed the dog a piece of bacon. Four hours later the dog died from pancreatic necrosis, an apparent reaction from the food. I have seen deadly reactions like this a number of times where pancreatic tissue literally becomes consumed by self-produced enzymes.

Catastrophic food-related episodes are not that common, but they do happen and when they do, as my clinical studies show, it is likely due to underlying endocrine-immune imbalances. My studies also show that more routine food allergies (also called food sensitivity or intolerance) occur only in animals with hormonal imbalances. They often develop reactions to certain foods as a result of constant exposure to the same food. If the diet is of particularly poor quality, reactions can develop quite early in life. Food sensitivities are less of a problem among cats than dogs.

Among other things, the typical pattern of endocrine-immune dysfunction significantly weakens IgA antibodies that have a paramount protective role in the mucous membranes of the body, including the intestinal tract where food breakdown takes place. Many other organs suffer as well because of this lost protection and become more susceptible to acute reactions and degeneration.

Food intolerances may involve one or more ingredient, or a particular combination of ingredients. Offensive substances can be anything from chemical additives, poor sources of protein, carbohydrates such as rice or wheat, to otherwise wholesome and nourishing foods. The eye-opening reality is that an animal with endocrine-immune imbalances can be intolerant even to natural, organic, or raw food. In some animals just a small amount of an offending food now and then is enough to trigger a reaction.

Pets with healthy hormones can usually eat the same diet for a lifetime without developing signs of sensitivity. However, an inferior diet of poor nutritional quality loaded with questionable chemical ingredients can certainly lead to a shorter, unhealthy life. Cheap products with poorly absorbed nutrients may cause diarrhea even in the hardiest of animals. Excessive defecation and voracious appetite are often signs of an inferior diet. There is also a possibility that impurities or deficiencies in such a diet could generate measurable endocrine and immune imbal-

The "HIT" List For Endocrine-Immune Defective Dogs

1. **Lamb.**
2. **Rice.**
3. **Milk.**
4. **Eggs.** Years ago, eggs were used in preparing distemper vaccines for dogs but they were dropped from formulations when it was found that they frequently caused reactions.
5. **Yeast and yeast-containing foods,** including brewer's yeast often given to animals for flea protection.
6. **Corn and corn oil.**
7. **Soybeans.**
8. **Pork.**
9. **Turkey.**
10. **Wheat and wheat byproducts,** when in combination with other allergens.
11. **Chicken**
12. **Beef and beef byproducts.**

ances that trigger food reactions. I have observed this a number of times over the years. These instances of acquired hormonal imbalances can usually be reversed with an improved diet.

Food allergies, sensitivities, or reactions may manifest as skin disorders, intestinal upset, vomiting and diarrhea, poor absorption of nutrients, or a variety of other ways. Remember that each animal is an individual. Two hypersensitive dogs or cats will probably react differently to the same food depending on their individual weaknesses and strengths.

During thirty years of treating animals with food-related disorders, I have created "HIT Lists" of major food offenders. HIT stands for "High In Trouble." These are the foods that are most problematic for animals. I have created three lists:

1) HIT foods for dogs with endocrine-immune imbalances;
2) HIT foods for cats with imbalances; and
3) HIT foods for dogs and cats without imbalances. You may have a dog or cat sensitive to any one or more of the listed foods.

My HIT lists may shock you. You may be thinking, There's nothing left to feed my animal. Please read on and do not despair. There is plenty of food for highly sensitive animals, you just have to learn what your pet can handle.

If you are a dog owner you cannot help but to have noticed that I put lamb and rice right at the top of the HIT list for food-sensitive canines. You probably think it is a safe hypoallergenic combination. It is not.

Let me explain. In the early 1980s I developed the first commercial lamb and rice formula for the original owners of Nature's Recipe. (The company was later sold.) I had previously formulated other special diets for food-sensitive animals for the company. These products were intended to provide a cleaner and more palatable food tolerated by the many animals who had become sensitized to the overexposure of beef by-products widely used in pet food. The thinking was that if you fed a food—such as lamb and rice—that animals were not used to eating, you could avoid or minimize food sensitivities. I took the idea of lamb and rice from the work of Albert Rowe, M.D., chief of the allergy clinic at the University of California Medical Center in San Francisco who decades earlier had successfully used this combination for food-sensitive children.

The "HIT" List For Endocrine-Immune Defective Cats

1. **Fish.**
2. **Milk and dairy products.**
3. **Yeast, yeast-containing foods,** and brewer's yeast.
4. **Corn and corn oil.**
5. **Pork.**
6. **Turkey.**
7. **Eggs.**
8. **Beef and beef byproducts.**
9. **Wheat and wheat byproducts** when in combination with other allergens.
10. **Chicken**

The concept worked for animals, too. The lamb and rice diet was indeed hypoallergenic because dogs had not been over exposed to these foods. Sensitive dogs could eat it and not react, or react much less than on standard formulations. The problem is that lamb and rice diets became too popular. Today there are about sixty versions of this combination on the market. Lamb and rice is everywhere, and increasingly animals have developed intolerance and reactions to these recipes just as they did in earlier years to beef-based diets. The sensitivity can possibly be explained in part as a result of the constant exposure to the lamb or rice, or it could be due to some individually offensive ingredient used in a particular formulation by the manufacturer. I have found that often an animal can tolerate one brand of lamb and rice but not another, so you have to wonder what else is in the other brand. Pet foods are highly processed with many chemicals and multiple ingredients, often of questionable purity, and any one of them could be a triggering agent.

The "HIT" List For Dogs and Cats Without Endocrine-Immune Imbalances

1. **Milk.** As many as 80 percent of pets, no matter what age, do not tolerate cow's milk (neither do many humans). After drinking it, they usually have gassy stomachs, vomiting, loose stool, or diarrhea. Raw, low fat, or nonfat milk—it does not matter. There is a much greater tolerance for cottage cheese, other cheeses, and yogurt.

2. **Turkey.** Following Thanksgiving and Christmas holidays veterinarians see a predictable influx of sick animals.

3. **Pork.** Too high in fat. This food can cause damaging reactions in the pancreas. One client fed her dog three strips of bacon every morning. It eventually killed the animal. An autopsy revealed an inflamed pancreas.

Interestingly, I have recently found that some dogs who now have developed sensitivity to lamb and rice can handle beef-based diets—at least for a while. This may be due simply to the fact that the animals have not been exposed much to beef in their lifetimes. If you decide to test beef tolerance, opt for as healthy a formula as possible. By that I mean a formula without chemical preservatives and with a beef source that has not been shot up with hormones.

Many health-oriented pet owners like to feed rice to their animals, particularly brown rice, which is more nutritious. Just be aware of the possibility that some pets may react to the rice whether it is white, brown, or basmati.

Similar to lamb and rice, soy used to be a fine source of protein, but I found that many animals with imbalances can not handle soybeans when exposed to them for a given period of time. Tofu, the fermented soy product, is less of a problem but nevertheless some animals are sensitive to it. Soy contains phytoestrogens, which are plant-based estrogen compounds. Feeding soy could possibly contribute to an estrogen excess or even worsen an already existing estrogen overload.

In order to help endocrine-immune imbalanced animals with fewer good options, I later developed "limited antigen diets" based on combinations of potatoes and protein sources that animals had little exposure to, and were therefore less likely to create food reactions. Testing validated the concept, leading to the creation of a new line of dry and canned foods for dogs and cats. Each item has just two ingredients: a protein source such as duck, rabbit, or venison, mixed with potatoes. We found that animals tend to be less sensitive to white potatoes than rice.

These products still need to be rotated periodically. Of course, you can also choose to cook for your pet if you have the time. That way you will know exactly what is in the mix.

Intolerance to foods is a result of endocrine-immune dysfunction. In the digestive tract, uncontrolled immune cells challenge food components as foreign invaders, setting off a whole scenario of upset, irritation, inflammation, and malabsorption, resulting in lessened ability to extract essential nutrients from the food. As genetic defects proliferate, more and more animals tolerate fewer and fewer foods. Increasingly, I find more pets than ever before in this sad shape. Some severely affected animals have hardly any safe food options. The bottom line is that the food sensitivities are secondary to the imbalances.

A good diet is a crucial part of the therapy program. In Chapter Ten, I explain why and describe how you can support the therapy and rehabilitation process with a protective diet.

Fleas and Other Pests

Healthy animals just do not seem to attract fleas. I have noticed this for years and heard the same comment from other veterinarians. Fleas appear to target weaker pets. In households with multiple pets, clients often tell me that a flea problem involves only one of their animals. The others, if bitten, are not reacting or reacting minimally.

For many years I have managed a wildlife refuge on my property. I see this same situation among wild animals, whether deer, raccoons, bobcats, coyotes, or rabbits. Weaker animals always seem full of fleas, ticks, and parasites. Stronger animals are much less affected.

If there is a major flea buildup in your immediate area, that is a different matter. In such a situation there may be so many fleas around that they jump on anything that moves. You know you have a serious problem when the fleas start biting your feet and ankles. If there is no such infestation, and the fleas are basically targeting a particular dog or cat, you can bet that the particular animal has a hormonal imbalance.

Dogs or cats with chronic flea reactions are out of balance. The endocrine-immune defect is disabling and prevents an animal from effectively counteracting the antigen—the offending protein in the flea saliva. Correcting the hormonal defect usually eliminates the reactivity problem.

As for treating animals suffering from fleas, I am wary of chemicalized anti-flea products that are applied topically or given orally to pets. I am concerned that these compounds may damage the endocrine-immune integrity of animals. Despite all the product guarantees about safety, I have traced cases of allergies, generalized mange, severe acute reactions, cancer, and even death to the use of chemical flea products.

I recommend testing an animal's endocrine-immune levels before initiating any pharmaceutical anti-flea preparation. If the levels are off, according to the values I detail in Chapter Eight, I would be reluctant to use the product. If a pet owner still uses the chemical product, I suggest retesting the animal's endocrine-immune levels to determine if any negative changes occur.

My experience with other pests is similar to that of fleas. Ear mites, for example, collect on dogs and cats producing excess earwax due to inflammation in the ears. This generally relates to an endocrine-immune imbalance. You may have several animals at home. One has ear mites, but the others do not. You might think the problem is contagious. It is not. The mites head for the animal with the excess earwax, and that is usually the one with the endocrine-immune imbalance.

Environmental Allergens

The endocrine-immune imbalance increases the potential for reactivity to environmental compounds and organisms that would otherwise not cause problems. Harmless substances for healthy animals become allergens for imbalanced pets.

Years ago, I developed a test that included seventy-five different allergen groupings to determine the specific intolerances of individual animals. I eventually discarded the test. It became clear that correcting the imbalance was more important than knowing each and every offending substance.

Endocrine-immune therapy usually and significantly reduces the sensitivity of an animal. A system in balance has a much greater capacity to handle potential stressors coming from the environment.

Environmental Toxins

The chemical revolution has given us countless benefits, but at the same time has exposed us to an unprecedented onslaught of new compounds with the potential to harm both humans and animals alike. An article in the April 2003 issue of *Smithsonian* describes changes in immune cells, antibodies, and hormones among Arctic polar bears that have scientists worried. The changes are a result of industrial chemicals called polychlorinated biphenyl compounds (PCBs) contaminating the marine food chain. Such chemicals can weaken the immune system with devastating results. For example, a distemper virus killed some 20,000 PCB-laden seals in Europe in 1988. These events and continual warnings from wildlife experts remind us that chemicals pose real threats to the health of planetary life.

According to Doris Rapp, M.D., a past president of the American Academy of Environmental Medicine and author of *Is This Your Child's World?* (Bantam Books, 1996), "Unless our nutrition is good we (humans) can not hope to detoxify these things. But our nutrition has deteriorated over the last half-century and we are no longer the robust, hardy people we used to be. We never had as much cancer as now. We never had Alzheimer's. We didn't see babies you couldn't breast-feed. Teachers will tell you they never had the behavioral problems years ago they are now having. The food we eat is processed, pesticided, and poor in nutrients. What we drink is full of chemicals. The result is that our bodies have become toxic dump sites."

Maybe cats and dogs do not develop Alzheimer's, but they certainly develop signs of chemical overload. With their noses close to the ground and carpets, our pets are intimately exposed to a multitude of toxins: lawn and garden compounds, rat poison, pesticides, cleaning and disinfectant solutions, lead in paint and water, building and decorating chemicals, and the fumes outgassing from synthetic carpets. Of course, there is the highly processed commercial pet food they eat, spiked with an A to Z of chemical additives.

Sensitive animals can develop an endless combination of mild to severe symptoms. Anything is possible, from allergic-like reactions to epileptic seizures. An existing endocrine-immune defect will render an animal even less able to cope with chemical challenges. The defect interferes with thyroid function, which can potentially slow down the metabolic process and hamper the body's ability to eliminate waste products. Waste remains in an animal's system longer, and undermines health and function. Toxins that enter the body are also processed less efficiently, potentially leading to further harm.

Chemicals also have the potential to cause an endocrine-immune problem. Philip Harvey, a leading British toxicologist and author of *The Adrenals in Toxicity: Target Organ and Modulator of Toxicity* (Taylor & Francis, 1996), states that the adrenal glands are more vulnerable to toxins than any other organ in the endocrine system. Within the adrenal gland, he adds, the majority of damage has been observed in the cortex and such disturbances can "fundamentally affect the whole body physiology and biochemistry." In an article in a 2002 issue of the *Journal of Applied Toxicology*, Harvey points out that the entire process of adrenal hormones "poses multiple molecular targets" for disruption due to toxicity.

My clinical observations over many years suggest that indeed the adrenal cortex is a prime target for toxic damage, and specifically the zona fasciculata of the cortex where cortisol is produced. I have seen many cases of cortisol deficiencies develop as an apparent result of exposure to environmental chemicals such as pesticides, anti-flea preparations, and anesthesia compounds. Such exposures have caused both short-term and permanent imbalances.

Vaccination Problems

Although vaccines are rigorously tested for efficacy and safety, no vaccine can really be considered 100 percent effective or safe. Experts say that weaknesses and differences in individual immune systems account for those occasions when people, or animals, are left unprotected after immunization or when they develop adverse side effects. Animal and human studies suggest that vaccinations are among the many genetic and environmental contributors to an increase in allergic disease.

Animals receive a variety of vaccines, either in combination or individually. Such vaccines include the following:

- Dogs—distemper, hepatitis, parvovirus, corona, rabies, leptospirosis, and kennel cough.
- Cats—feline distemper, rhinotracheitis, pneumonitis, feline leukemia, feline infectious peritonitis, and rabies if animals live in an area with a known rabies incidence.

Reactions are not uncommon, although many veterinarians tend to downplay such events. Adverse effects have actually been increasing because of the use of multiple antigens and the hypersensitivity potential for reactions among genetically susceptible animals according to a 1995 article in the *Journal of the American Veterinary Medical Association.*

Most easily identifiable reactions occur within twenty-four hours. They range from hive-like urticarial swelling, facial edema, and lethargy, to acute anaphylaxis, bronchial spasm, loss of blood pressure, rapid heart rate, and even death. However, reactions could take much longer to develop—weeks, months, or even years.

From my clinical experience, the hormonal imbalances I have identified in so many cases of immune incompetence are routinely present in pets with a history of vaccination reactions, failure to develop anticipated immunity, or who contract the actual disease against which they were specifically inoculated. If the hormones are normal, these problems usually do not occur.

If the defect is present, the body may not be able to tolerate or process a vaccine correctly, even if the vaccine itself is of the so-called modified (killed cell) variety that cannot cause disease.

The combination of low cortisol and elevated estrogen interferes with thyroid function in a number of ways. The metabolism slows and the vaccine may remain in the system for much longer than normal before it is eventually processed out. This gives a deranged immune system more exposure—and more reaction time—to the vaccine. The vaccines act as actual allergens instead of protective agents to stimulate the immune system.

There is yet another issue here. Veterinarians are instructed by vaccine manufacturers to administer the same quantity of a vaccine to a small or large dog. Thus a three-pound Yorkie will get the same dosage that a huge Saint Bernard gets. If both animals have the same degree of endocrine-immune imbalance, guess which one will react more severely? That is a phenomenal amount of toxic input for a small dog to process, especially if the animal has a deranged immune system.

Blood tests known as antibody titers have become available to veterinarians to determine the strength of an animal's immune system and in particular assess the response of the system to vaccinations. Titer scores below normal mean a pet lacks protection and is still vulnerable.

If an animal does not develop antibodies, as determined by titer tests, or develops an adverse reaction, or gets the same disease he or she was vaccinated for, consider the presence of endocrine-immune imbalances. Once corrected, there are usually no more vaccination failures.

In cats, be alert for any growths at the site of a vaccination injection. A harmless swelling frequently occurs and usually disappears after several weeks. But a cancerous growth called fibrosarcoma sometimes develops exactly where animals receive multiple inoculations. This growth is locally aggressive, invasive, tends to recur, and can be fatal. If you notice any growth at the site, contact your veterinarian immediately.

In my practice I always administer the injections in different parts of the body to prevent the problem. I believe that the quantity of the injected material alone in one spot is capable of setting off an uncontrolled reaction. I also believe that a deranged immune system could promote a systemic reaction as well.

The following case histories demonstrate how the testing and treatment method I have developed can help resolve routine vaccination complications.

Harlequin Dane female puppy, twelve weeks old

The people who owned this puppy had previously lost another dog to a parvovirus infection despite having done the routine immunizations with another veterinarian. The vaccines apparently had not produced antibody protection.

The new puppy, named Gwenevere, weighed fifteen pounds when I first saw her. She had been obtained from a rescue organization where she had already been vaccinated twice. The owners brought the dog in for her distemper and parvovirus shots.

"Can you guarantee us that she will not break with something communicable, even though she's been vaccinated?" they asked.

"No," I said. "You need to let me measure her antibody titers first and see if the vaccine works and her system produces antibodies. The reality is that many animals who are vaccinated do not get any benefit from the shots. They just do not produce the antibodies."

I proceeded with a titer test for parvovirus and distemper to determine if the previous vaccinations had been effective. The test showed that no antibodies had been produced.

I then recommended an endocrine-immune blood test. The results showed the dog had low cortisol, high total estrogen, suppressed thyroid hormones, and low IgA, IgG, and IgM. The B cells were not responding to the vaccinations.

I initiated a program of low-dosage cortisone and thyroid replacement. I rechecked the puppy after two weeks to see if the program needed modification. The blood values had significantly improved, and indicated to me that a revaccination series would be effective. After completion of the series, I did another titer test. Indeed, the results showed a healthy antibody response. Gwenevere has remained on the therapy program for more than two-and-a-half-years without any health problems.

I have had numerous cases where new clients brought in dogs who previously had been vaccinated for parvo yet still contracted the disease. "It must be a different strain," they said to me, repeating what they were told. My response has usually been that it is not a different strain, it is the endocrine-immune imbalances preventing normal antibody production from the vaccines.

Female Siamese cat, spayed, fifteen months old

The cat's owner, a new client, told me that her pet had almost died from a severe reaction immediately after the first kitten immunization, a multiple vaccine, and had not been vaccinated since. I recommended an endocrine-immune blood panel. The results indicated endocrine-immune imbalance. I started a replacement program of low-dosage cortisone. After two weeks, I rechecked the cat. The results were normal.

Around this time, the client had decided to board the cat temporarily in a cattery. To do so required immunization with the same multiple vaccine the animal had received earlier. I re-vaccinated the cat and monitored her closely. No immediate or subsequent reactions took place. The cat was boarded without any problem.

Male Pug, three years old

The dog had a repeated history of vomiting and diarrhea within hours after vaccinations. Another veterinarian administered an anti-emetic with vaccinations so as to minimize reactions.

The dog had developed a food allergy and was referred to my clinic. An endocrine-immune panel revealed a typical profile of imbalance. I corrected it with low-dosage cortisone and thyroid and then re-vaccinated the dog. For a day I kept him under observation in the clinic. There were no vomiting, diarrhea, or other adverse reactions. The dog's food sensitivity problem also resolved. The dog has been maintained regularly on the same therapy for about nine years and has had no vaccination reactions during that time.

What Is Ahead?

You have now read about the many problems created by widespread endocrine-immune imbalances in pets that are not familiar to most veterinarians. In the chapters ahead I explain the practical steps involved in identifying these health-destroying imbalances and how to correct them.

Part Two

THE SOLUTION

– SEVEN –

Repairing Endocrine-Immune Imbalances

In the early 1970s I was fortunate to figure out why many of my canine and feline patients were getting sick and dying prematurely. The testing and treatment program I developed put me in the business of repairing defective endocrine-immune pets and it has worked magnificently for thousands of animals. Over the years I honed the program as I continued learning from my patients and from research into the complexities of hormones and immune interactions. Throughout all this, one key ingredient for success has not changed: commitment.

Commitment means cooperation between the veterinarian and the patient's human caregiver. Commitment also means staying the course. It is a partnership. Your veterinarian performs the necessary testing and medical services. You provide the necessary home care and monitoring, and return for follow-up visits as needed. Once an animal's endocrine-immune system has been adjusted, a long-term maintenance program requires amazingly little effort on your part. But it is a long-term program.

An animal with endocrine-immune imbalances usually gets better quickly; however, you cannot stop the program once you see improvement and recovery. You are dealing with a hormonal defect, not a simple bacterial infection that is cured after a ten-day course of antibiotics. The program I have developed compensates for a physiological deficiency with medication that acts as a hormone replacement. If you stop the medication, signs of illness will return. The defect is generally of a permanent nature. This usually means giving your animal a pill a day and feeding a nutritious diet that does not contain offending foods.

If you make this commitment, you will be part of a powerful healing program that transforms sick animals and keeps them healthy. Used preventively, this program can also head off future disease in adrenally defective animals.

Karla Champion, one of my clients for many years, knows how well the program works. I have treated ten of her dogs starting with Annie, a young but very sick Yorkie-mixed breed dog adopted from a rescue organization. The endocrine-immune balance program restored Annie's health and maintained her for the rest of her life. She lived to be thirteen.

"Annie would never have made it without this program," Karla says. "The experience was so positive that I decided my puppies should all get tested. Some needed therapy, others didn't. I decided that those who needed the therapy would get the necessary retesting, adjustments, good food, and periodic checkups. It has been a commitment on my part but it has paid off with the super good health for my animals. I know of other dogs from the same litters who have had lots of health problems."

The Endocrine-Immune Program

Step One Your pet needs a simple blood test to enable your veterinarian to identify the presence of critical imbalances. In Chapter Eight I provide the guidelines on how to recognize these imbalances from test results. While the information is intended primarily for veterinarians, I invite health-conscious pet owners to read it in order to better understand the importance of the testing process.

Step Two If imbalances are found, Chapter Nine contains the specific instructions for your veterinarian to start a safe and effective hormone replacement program. I include instructions on how to adjust medication, switch to a natural form of cortisone, schedule periodic checkups, and deal with contingencies that may arise. The detailed guidelines are meant for veterinarians, but I strongly recommend pet owners to familiarize themselves with the main points of the therapy program.

Step Three Simultaneously with the start of therapy, animals should be put on a special but simple diet that eliminates potentially offending foods. Diet is a very important element in ensuring the success of the program. In Chapter Ten I advise pet owners on how to create a healthy and supportive dietary plan that meets the individual needs of their animals.

Step Four Selected supplements can enhance the therapy and healing process. The supplement program begins with digestive enzymes to help break down food and enhance absorption. I explain this in Chapter Eleven.

Step Five Careful consideration of preventive measures. Chapter Fourteen discusses preventive measures, including information on how to examine your pet for signs of imbalances and other indicators of ill health.

Step Six This step, covered in Chapter Fifteen, is for breeders. Ultimately, disease prevention and stopping the proliferation of endocrine-immune dysfunction depends upon breeders choosing healthy—and not just fashionable—animals for breeding. If you know breeders, or have obtained your animal from a breeder, bring this book to their attention. You will be advancing the cause of healthier generations of future dogs and cats.

Costs of the Program

There are a couple of considerations regarding the cost of the endocrine-immune testing and the long-term hormone replacement program. Keep in mind that the blood test price varies from laboratory to laboratory, as do treatment costs from veterinarian to veterinarian. Basically, I can report only the arrangements in my clinic.

Many of my first-time patients are extremely sick animals in crisis with catastrophic diseases. That is because pet owners often come to me as a last resort. In critical cases, I have to decide on an immediate therapeutic program to enable the patient to survive. Although I draw blood for the endocrine-immune test, I do not have the luxury of waiting for test results.

At the time of publication in 2003, the charge in my clinic for the initial blood test and laboratory results was $225 to $250. This fee does not include the cost for the initial office call with examination. After two weeks on the program, and the condition of the pet has improved, I do a second blood test. The second test helps determine if modifications of hormone replacement dosages are needed. In some serious cases I may suggest a third test after a month or more in order to fine-tune the program. Generally, I suggest retesting only at yearly intervals, whenever pets show signs of health changes, or when pet owners have some particular concern.

Patients are maintained long-term on cortisol replacement medication—either natural or synthetic—depending on the case. Most dogs, and a small percentage of cats, also require maintenance on thyroid medication. The cost of such daily oral medication varies according to the size of the animal. In my clinic, daily cortisol replacement pills may range from about ten cents a day for a small dog or cat up to a dollar a day for a large dog. Price may also vary depending on which cortisol replacement is used. Thyroid pills run from about ten cents to forty cents a day.

A few patients cannot be sustained on oral cortisol replacement medication and require long-acting cortisone injections on a monthly basis. The charge in my clinic to administer once-a-month injections is $40. That includes the actual medication and staff time. If clients are interested and want to save on extra costs, I instruct them on how to inject their pets at home. Done at home, the cost of the medication and syringes ranges from $10 to $15 per injection.

If a client does not want to administer the shots, we offer them another money-saving option where we sell them syringes and a vial of appropriate medication good for several injections. The pet owner returns with the pet each month and brings the syringes and medication to the clinic. A staff technician or I then administer the injection at a much-reduced charge.

Before You Start

- If your animal companion suffers from a major health problem, be sure to seek professional help first before trying anything on your own.
- Do not stop any treatment that has been prescribed for your cat or dog by a veterinarian. Consult with your veterinarian. Discuss the ideas presented in this book as a fresh approach, or a possible addition to ongoing therapy, or as an alternative to standard procedures that may not be yielding good results.

EIGHT

The Test that Can Make a Difference

T he special blood test I have developed identifies the key, out-of-sync elements of endocrine-immune imbalances. There are four versions of the test:

1) **The basic E-I One** test measures the levels of critical hormone and immune factors: cortisol, total estrogen, the thyroid hormones T-3 and T-4, and IgA, IgM, and IgG antibodies.
2) **The E-I Two** test is a combination of the E-I One test plus the standard complete blood count (CBC) and blood chemistry panels. This broader test provides a comprehensive picture of how endocrine-immune imbalances may negatively impact blood cells and organs.
3) **The E-I Three** test measures only hormone levels and is intended for young puppies and kittens only.
4) **The E-I Four** test adds Von Willebrand's disease factor to the basic E-I One test.

At present, the tests are available through the following laboratories:
- National Veterinary Diagnostic Services
  Phone: (877) VETS LAB (838-7522)
  Website: www.national-vet.com
- IDEXX Laboratory Services
  Phone: (800) 444-4210
  Website: www.idexx.com
- Antech Diagnostics
  Phone: (800) 872-1001 (East), (800) 745-4725 (West)
  Website: www.antechdiagnostics.com

The tests are based on simple blood draws. After the draw at the veterinary clinic, a technician spins down the blood in a serum separator tube and refrigerates it. It is shipped cold and refrigerated at the lab until testing. If blood is not kept cold, results will be invalid, showing excessively high ranges. For specific shipment details, veterinarians should contact the laboratory directly.

How to Interpret Test Results

I base my interpretation of endocrine-immune tests primarily on comparisons of the key hormones and antibodies. Their relationships with each other tell me much more than just reading individual values. For instance, looking at cortisol and thyroid levels by themselves is quite meaningless when you realize that the numbers do not reflect active, working hormone concentrations. Individual values include both active and inactive constituents of the hormones, and the inactive portions are huge. For instance, something in the order of 0.1 percent of thyroxine, one of the thyroid hormones, is actually free or unbound and actively working in the system. Proteins in the blood bind up the preponderance of the circulating hormone. Because of such peculiarities of hormonal physiology, I focus on the whole constellation of levels and their relationships to each other. This assessment tells me if the hormones are working or not.

The initial blood test serves as a baseline measurement of the defective endocrine-immune mechanism. If hormone and antibody levels are slightly outside of normal ranges there may not be clear signs of disease. From a preventive standpoint I recommend rechecking blood levels again within six months to a year due to the typically progressive nature of endocrine-immune imbalances. They tend to get worse with time and, as a consequence of continuing immune system deregulation, increasing evidence of disease. When used in this manner the test provides an excellent early detection method.

Furthermore, the results allow me to make a direct assessment of a patient's health status. The more pronounced the imbalances, the more advanced the disease process. For instance, an animal with an autoimmune condition or cancer has hormone and antibody levels far out of the normal range. In the case of older animals, however, I generally find that even a slight abnormality may

Endocrine-Immune "Normal" Values for Dogs and Cats

Important note for the veterinarian: The reference ranges I developed and have used for many years are based on my clinical experience. They may vary widely from ranges set by different laboratories. **For maximum results when following my therapy program use only the measurements below.** Be sure to specify the appropriate **Plechner Endocrine-Immune Test** to the laboratory.

CORTISOL	1-2.5 ug/dl
T3	100-200 ng/dl
T4	2-4.5 ug/dl
IgA	70-170 mg/dl
IgG	1,000-2,000 mg/dl
IgM	100-200 mg/dl

Male Estrogen Level

TOTAL ESTROGEN	20-25 pg/ml

Female Estrogen Level*

TOTAL ESTROGEN	30-35 PG/ML

■ Results that are lower or higher typically indicate the presence of imbalances and accompanying health problems.

■ The hormone values apply to dogs and cats of all ages.

■ The antibody values apply to animals above the age of six months, or a month after their last round of puppy and kitten shots. Antibody levels in younger animals may be suppressed, and not represent true values because of the impact of vaccines on immature immune systems.

* The female range is for spayed or out-of-heat animals. If a female is in heat, it is difficult to obtain a true reading for total estrogen because of the presence of ovarian estrogen.

create a marked medical effect. The chart above lists the normal test measurements I find associated with good health.

How to Interpret the Cortisol Level

Physical, emotional, and environmental stresses affect the production and utilization of cortisol. Once secreted by the adrenal cortex into the blood, certain proteins (corticosteroid-binding globulin and albumin) bind up approximately 90 percent of the cortisol hormone. The bound cortisol circulates in an inactive, reserve status for use by the body when needed. The multiple physiological functions of cortisol depend upon the small fraction of circulating active cortisol.

The endocrine-immune tests measure total serum cortisol in the serum. (Previously, cortisol was measured in the plasma.) But the number by itself does not really indicate whether the circulating cortisol is active, bound, or defective, and how much of it actually works. The important question is whether cortisol works or not.

The answer comes from analyzing the other hormonal and antibody measurements. A low cortisol reading on the test, along with elevated estrogen and low antibodies, is a clear indication of endocrine-immune imbalances. However, you may see a normal value for cortisol. Nevertheless, if accompanied by an estrogen level higher than normal and antibody scores lower than normal, you are dealing with cortisol that is excessively bound or defective. The result is the same. Defective or deficient cortisol promotes elevated estrogen. This in turn contributes to deregulation of the immune system, resulting in low antibody levels.

A high cortisol score is regarded as Cushing's syndrome. However, understand that even a high cortisol value may give a false portrayal of an excessively inactive or bound hormone in large part not utilized by the body. Confirmation would be an accompanying complete blood count showing normal amounts of eosinophils and lymphocytes (immune system cells). In a true case of Cushing's, a genuine hypersecretion of active cortisol suppresses lymphocytes and eosinophils (lymphopenia and eosinopenia) and creates a low total estrogen level.

The total estrogen level in the endocrine-immune tests also tells you whether the cortisol level represents a real hypersecretion of active cortisol or not. High estrogen means an excessively bound or defective concentration of cortisol, and not Cushing's syndrome. If this were indeed the case, administration of Lysodren, the standard treatment for Cushing's, would severely hurt an animal. Lysodren destroys adrenal cortical tissue. This is how the cortisol level is brought down to a more normal range. However, if you further suppress an already defective cortisol mechanism you run the risk of further damage and perhaps even killing the animal.

Over the years I have found an extremely high level of bound cortisol in about seventy-five dogs. I successfully treated them with low, physiologic doses of cortisone. If the cortisol was not excessively bound or defective in some way, this hormonal replacement strategy would obviously be contra-indicated.

On a related note: if blood chemistry shows normal levels of sodium and potassium, this indicates that the outer layer of the adrenal cortex is producing enough of the mineralocorticoid aldosterone. This is the hormone that regulates those critical electrolytes. I see no discernible role of the outer adrenal cortical layer and aldosterone in the typical pattern of endocrine-immune imbalances. A deficiency of mineralocorticoid hormone is associated with Addison's disease. The defect I am concerned with involves defective or deficient cortisol, a problem originating in the middle layer of the cortex, and does not seem to involve aldosterone.

Estrogen Interpretation

Standard tests measure only one estrogen compound: estradiol. The endocrine-immune test calls for a total measurement of all estrogen compounds, including estrone and estriol. The reason for a total estrogen reading is because the other compounds may be part of an estrogen buildup that contributes to destabilizing effects in the body.

Too much estrogen, for instance, has a binding effect on both cortisol and the thyroid hormones. These hormones may show up as perfectly normal in a test, yet they may be inactivated to some physiologically significant degree by estrogen. This phenomenon has not been adequately recognized.

A large percentage of the female animals I treat have been spayed. If you test a non-spayed female who is in heat, the estrogen level will likely be higher as it represents a combination of ovarian and adrenal-induced estrogen. For an intact female, always do the test after the estrus period. This can be easily determined by a vaginal smear.

Thyroid Interpretation (T3, T4)

The thyroid gland produces two principal hormones from the amino acid tyrosine and the mineral iodine. The hormones are named triiodotyronine, or T3 for short, and thyroxine, or T4. Most of the thyroid's secretion is T4, serving largely as a reserve for conversion, as needed by the body into the considerably more active T3 form. This process, called transference, requires an adequate level of cortisol. Deficient cortisol retards transference and cellular use of thyroid hormones, interactions not well recognized outside of the field of endocrinology.

Bound or deficient thyroid hormones result in a state of hypothyroidism requiring replacement medication. This situation exists in

90 percent of dogs with endocrine-immune imbalances, but only in a small percentage of cats.

The elevated estrogen I typically see in affected dogs binds both thyroid hormones. Testing may show normal thyroid levels, but in reality the hormones are disabled to varying degrees and not doing their jobs efficiently. Signs of insufficient thyroid include slow heart rate, low temperature, high cholesterol and triglycerides, lethargy, and bilateral hair loss. The presence of these signs overrides any normal thyroid test results.

Many times a T4 count appears very high with a low T3 level. This occurs as a result of not enough working cortisol to promote the normal transference of storage T4 to active T3.

Most veterinarians only test for T4. I regard this as a major mistake. When excess estrogen binds thyroid hormones, T4 is not broken down properly. You may thus see a high T4 test result. It means nothing. And if the cortisol is defective or deficient, you get the problem with transference of T4 to T3 and reduced cellular thyroid hormone effectiveness within cells.

Typically, hyperthyroid diagnoses in cats are made on the basis of a high T4 level alone, a result of impaired transference. In this situation, the diagnosis is inaccurate. The test for endocrine-immune imbalances provides a better diagnostic picture. Elevated estrogen and abnormal thyroid results indicate a primary problem with cortisol. Long-term treatment with low-dosage cortisone promises to be the answer rather than the use of Tapazole, a drug that kills thyroid tissue.

In dogs, a high T4 count often relates to a cortisol problem affecting transference as well as elevated estrogen binding the thyroid hormones.

Antibody Interpretation

The hormonal imbalances deregulate the immune cells that produce antibodies. Low IgA, IgG, and IgM counts on the endocrine-immune test turn up routinely in affected animals. The results reflect the malfunction going on in the immune system and the presence of immune-related problems.

Low antibodies suggest the possibility of a poor response to vaccinations. Frequently, imbalanced dogs and cats develop side effects or break out with the very diseases against which they have been inoculated.

Immunoglobulin A (IgA) has been of particular interest to m[ ]
a major yardstick in assessing disease and recovery. IgA is the most
abundant antibody and is especially important in mucosal immunity.
That means it functions as an essential protective factor against infectious agents, allergens, and foreign proteins that enter the body via
the mouth, nose, upper respiratory tract, the intestines, and reproductive tract.

In humans, where much more research has taken place, IgA deficiency is recognized as the most frequent immune system deficiency. In
animals, I routinely find a low IgA blood level in connection with malabsorption and inflammation in the intestinal tract. This results in
impaired nutrient absorption as well as an inability of patients to absorb
medication such as cortisone. A blood test score below 60 mg/dl suggests the presence of malabsorption.

I also find low IgA in gingival buccal inflammation, glossitis,
esophagitis, gastric enteritis, and food sensitivities. Outside of the digestive tract I routinely see IgA deficiency as a regular backdrop to the following problems:

- Respiratory tract—rhinitis, hayfever, pharyngitis,
  pneumonitis, and asthma.
- Inflammatory conditions of the kidneys, bladder,
  and urethra. Often kidney and bladder stones are
  consequences of the imbalance.
- Reproductive-tract inflammation of the uterus,
  ovaries, vagina.
- Miscarriage.
- Inflammatory joint disorders such as rheumatoid
  arthritis.
- Vaccine reactions.

Kittens and Puppies

The E-I Three test is designed for kittens and puppies. A simple
modification of the E-I One test, it excludes antibody counts. The reason for this is because antibody values may not be accurate due to the
influence of recent vaccines.

The E-I Three test identifies genetic hormonal imbalances. The
greater the degree of imbalance, the greater the loss of control over the
immune system and an early presentation of health problems.

Cortisol, T3, T4, and estrogen are genetically pre-determined. These are what can—and should—be measured in kittens and puppies as young as six to eight weeks of age. The "normal" values are the same as I listed earlier in the chapter.

I use this test for two purposes:

1) To screen for possible hormonal imbalances in a pet before a person acquires a particular animal. If the test shows such an imbalance, the potential owner can then make an educated decision whether to accept a genetically damaged animal or not. Keeping such an animal healthy over a lifetime will usually require long-term hormonal replacement.

2) To identify hormonal imbalances when antibody titer test results are unsatisfactory. After the last series of puppy/kitten immunizations, usually around ten to twelve weeks of age, I suggest running an antibody titer test. Results indicating less than adequate protection mean that the animal has not responded sufficiently to the vaccines. The E-I Three test is appropriate at this point. It will very likely show hormonal imbalances, which is why the vaccines have not worked.

The hormonal replacement procedures in Chapter Nine correct the imbalances. Two weeks after starting the therapy I repeat the E-I Three test. If the values are normal, vaccinations can be administered again. Two weeks afterward recheck the antibody titers. Usually, the counts show that the antibody protection is there. This scenario indicates that the animal should be kept on a hormone replacement program for life.

Older Animals

Aging of the hormone-producing organs generates health problems in the later years of life just as purely genetic defects trigger problems earlier on. The aging process causes hormonal slowdown and imbalances throughout the system.

The specific cortisol-based endocrine-immune imbalances I see in animals produces premature aging. I thus regard testing of animals and correcting imbalances if they exist, as good anti-aging medicine. The E-I One test may be used at any point in life, even among older animals. I have successfully applied the endocrine-immune program to pets as old as sixteen years of age, which enhanced their quality of life.

NINE

The Hormone Replacement Program

Once the endocrine-immune test has determined the presence of imbalances the next step is to launch an effective hormone replacement program. For most dogs, that means low-dosage cortisone medication to correct the cortisol deficiency, along with a thyroid supplement. For cats, the program usually calls for cortisone alone, except for felines who have infectious peritonitis (FIP) or a hypothyroid condition. In these cases, they, too, require a thyroid supplement.

The therapy program has two goals:
1) To eliminate current signs of illness by correcting the identified imbalances;
2) To sustain long-term health. Most affected animals require low-dosage cortisone for a lifetime.

Replacing Cortisol

I believe in very conservative dosages of cortisone to replace the deficient cortisol. I use just enough medication to correct the deficiency and bring estrogen and the immune cells back into a state of healthy functioning. The operative term here is physiologic dosage. By that I mean an amount quite a bit lower than the standard treatment levels used by veterinarians.

First Phase: Approximately Two weeks

General starting oral dosages are as follows:
- Medrol or Prednisone: 1 milligram per 10 pounds of body weight.
- Vetalog: .125 milligrams per 10 pounds.

These are daily oral dosages for noncritical animals. Critical cases or catastrophic diseases will likely require intravenous drips or intramuscular injections in the beginning. I explain my protocol for these situations in the section on malabsorption later in the chapter.

The recommended starting dosages are designed to begin correcting the body's deficiency without generating cortisone side effects such as incontinence, lethargy, panting at night, hair loss, retention of water, and excess drinking, urination, or eating. And most importantly, without further suppressing the immune system.

For dogs, my preferences are Medrol or Vetalog. For cats, Prednisone. However, each practitioner may have his or her preference, based on experience. Signs of side effects could occur in some cases as a result of a particular animal's individual aversion to a specific form of cortisone medication. This can be addressed by switching to another form. Medrol, for instance, may work better for one animal and Vetalog for another.

Occasionally, I find that any form of cortisone, even at low, physiologic doses, causes discomfort and side effects. I am usually able to resolve the problem and achieve clinical control with a "50-50 approach." By that I mean using two cortisol replacements—each at half the low dosage listed above. I have successfully applied this same strategy when an animal rejects a particular thyroid preparation. Two smaller dosages of different medications seem to be tolerated in animals who otherwise cannot take either one by itself.

In recent years I have used a natural cortisone product made from soy, and have had excellent long-term results. I describe my use of natural cortisone later in this chapter.

Second Phase: Modifying Dosage after Two Weeks

A second endocrine-immune blood test is done in two weeks. The results of the second test dictate whether to stay with the initial dosage or make a modification.

Compare the new values to the normal ranges listed in the previous chapter and to the animal's original baseline levels. See how much the values have moved toward normal. Insignificant changes call for a higher dosage of cortisone at this point. If the changes have moved fairly well towards normal, then stay with the same dosage or perhaps increase slightly. The desired remedial pattern veterinarians want to see is as follows: elevated estrogen dropping down into the normal range and low antibody levels rising. Of course, vets will take into consideration the clinical signs. Health improvements typically accompany better test scores.

Each patient is biochemically different and should be viewed individually. From my perspective, one key difference is the amount of active working cortisol produced by the adrenal glands. One animal, minimally deficient, may respond to 1 milligram of cortisone. The next animal—same size, same breed—may have a more severe deficiency, and require 5 or 10 milligrams in order to normalize the deficiency.

I have encountered many situations where a very large dog needed less cortisone than a much smaller dog. As an example, I corrected a 140-pound Saint Bernard whose endocrine-immune imbalances were quite pronounced with only 1 milligram of Medrol. I have no doubt that a higher dosage would have caused side effects. Yet, the same day I corrected a Shih Tzu, weighing 14 pounds, with 2 milligrams.

The same situation pertains to cats. I may treat a 22-pounder with 2.5 milligrams of Prednisone, and a 10-pounder with 10 milligrams. The important thing to remember is to treat animals individually and use the test results and clinical signs as guidelines. Increase or decrease dosages accordingly.

Use the lowest possible amount of cortisone in order to correct the deficiency and give the body its missing equivalency of cortisol. The therapy restores normal cortisol feedback to the pituitary, and stops the constant ACTH stimulation of adrenal estrogen. This corrective action—addressing the deficiency and subsequently decreasing estrogen—brings order back to a dysfunctional immune system.

Third Phase: The Long Term

Staying on the program is the key to success. It is a long-term proposition, not a short-term therapy.

Archie, a big orange tabby cat was maintained for a lifetime on 10 milligrams of Prednisone from six months of age. And what a lifetime! He lived to be twenty-eight! Archie was quite a do-gooder. He would roam the neighborhood and bring home stray kittens. Over the years he brought in eight of them and "mothered" them temporarily until his caregivers could bring the strays in to my hospital. Then we found homes for them.

Cortisone Every Other Day?

Over the years, many veterinarians have contacted me about my protocol. Some have prescribed the cortisone every other day instead of daily and wondered why clinical signs did not improve or were returning.

Understandably, such reluctance to use cortisone as I recommend is usually based on the fear that cortisone therapy suppresses the immune system. However, well-measured physiologic dosages do not suppress immune cells in cortisol-defective animals. As I have written before, the therapy restores orderliness to the immune system and the system then functions as Nature designed it to work. In almost all cases, deficient animals need daily replacement.

I also had a Dachshund named Dale who went on therapy at about six months. He lived to be twenty-seven. Dale and Archie are my Methuselah poster pets. Obviously, not every dog or cat can make it that long, but the vast majority of patients live much longer and healthier lives on this therapy.

Once the blood levels appear normal and clinical signs diminish, it is important for pet owners to bring their animal companions back for retesting. Most return once a year, although in the beginning some may come back after three or six months.

Usually there are no problems until a patient gets much older or undergoes a traumatic event, such as surgery or an accident. At such times clinicians should recheck the hormone and antibody levels again to make sure there have not been any changes.

An animal taken off the therapy will usually develop clinical signs of illness again. I have seen this happen numerous times because pet owners simply did not believe me when I said their animals needed to stay on the program for a lifetime. Often they were influenced by another veterinarian or someone else who assured them that cortisone therapy would shorten the life of their pet.

Pet owners have been told things like "cortisone is bad," "you cannot keep your animal on cortisone indefinitely," or "you're killing your animal." I certainly understand the fear of cortisone therapy. But I use cortisone to correct a cortisol deficiency causing major health problems. The low level physiologic dosage does not cause side effects. The medication compensates for a deficiency, restores hormonal balance, and brings back order to the immune system. If you stop the therapy, signs of the deficiency will recur. I have seen relapses repeatedly.

Other veterinarians who routinely use my method are very aware of this and encourage their clients to stay the course. Dwight Benesh, D.V.M., of Chandler, Arizona, states: "I've treated hundreds of animals with this therapy for ten years. As long as the pet owners cooperate, and follow the program, the results are very gratifying. If they stop the program, the original problems come back."

One common fear of extended cortisone therapy relates to the possibility of triggering an adrenal crisis if the medication is stopped at some point. An abrupt stop can indeed do that. If someone chooses to discontinue the program, the way to minimize or avoid a potential problem is to slowly wean the animal off the cortisone. For one week, reduce the daily dosage in half. Then, for the second week, use the half dosage every other day. This slowdown can avert an adrenal crisis, however, as a consequence of stopping the program you can expect health problems to start showing up fairly soon if the animal has the underlying cortisol deficiency. This should tell you that the animal cannot produce proper cortisol, and indeed requires long-term replacement with cortisone, and should stay on the program.

Unfortunately, and all too frequently, I have had to recommend this slowdown protocol to numerous clients who, despite the continuing good health of a once sick animal, were negatively influenced by other people. Some of these clients moved out of the area or transferred the care of their animals to other veterinarians not familiar with my research and the concept of low-dosage cortisone as a replacement for a deficient hormone. Unfortunately, this approach is not taught in veterinary schools. Some clients stopped the therapy without advising me. Afterwards, they called in a panic when their pet developed diarrhea, vomiting, or other signs of adrenal crisis.

Natural Cortisone for Long-Term Use

For more than five years I have utilized natural cortisone in capsule form made from soy. The product, referred to commonly as hydrocortisone, is an identical replica of the cortisol manufactured by the adrenal cortex. The liver apparently handles this natural form more easily than the synthetic pharmaceuticals.

If a presenting condition is not too serious I may use the natural product from the start. Otherwise I use it for long-term maintenance as soon as clinical signs and blood tests normalize. Once there is good improvement, I switch most patients to the hydrocortisone.

The clinician should recognize that the natural preparation does not work as fast as the synthetic cortisone drugs. With oral pharmaceuticals, you may see effects within two or three hours. Some injectables work within one hour. It takes five to seven days to create an effective loading dose with the natural medication. Since it takes this much time for the natural replacement to become fully "operational" in the body, I switch patients from the pharmaceutical cortisone in the following way:

- Start the pet on 1/2-milligram daily of natural hydrocortisone per 1 pound of body weight.
- Continue giving the pharmaceutical cortisone daily at the prescribed dosage for one week.
- On the seventh day, stop the pharmaceutical, and continue with the natural hydrocortisone.

If any signs of excess cortisone develop during the one-week switchover period—such as increased thirst or appetite, or panting at night—reduce the pharmaceutical cortisone to one-half the daily dosage. Such signs indicate that the natural product has kicked in earlier than expected. I have encountered this effect occasionally and usually only toward the very end of the transition period.

The natural medication also takes five days or so to "unload." This interval provides a safety factor. Much of the ingested natural cortisone gets stored in fat tissue. Slowly, the body draws on this stored supply as needed. Thus, if the animal's caregiver misses one or two days of administering the medication, there is usually not a problem. However, when pharmaceutical cortisone is stopped, or the pet owner forgets to administer it, a crisis could indeed occur.

The natural cortisone seems to maintain animals at least as well as the pharmaceuticals do and perhaps a bit better. However, a recurrence of the original signs of illness while using the natural product means that a pet has developed malabsorption. To remedy this, the veterinarian needs to revert to an injectable pharmaceutical cortisone. That should resolve the problem. (See the following section on malabsorption.)

Hydrocortisone is available as a prescription through compounding pharmacies that customize drugs, nutritional supplements, and natural hormones for medical practitioners and patients. The licensed pharmacists who work at compounding pharmacies mix, assemble, package, and label these preparations using high-quality, government-approved raw chemicals and natural substances. Some compounding pharmacies are part of drugstores where the usual commercial array of medications and household hygiene products are sold. Others specialize only in compounding activities. By comparison, the regular commercial pharmacy most people are familiar with primarily dispenses an already manufactured product.

I obtain hydrocortisone from Pet Health Pharmacy in Youngtown, Arizona (Phone: (800) 742-0516). Other compounding pharmacies also offer the product. As a prescription item, it can only be ordered by veterinary clinics. Pet owners cannot order directly.

Natural medication comes in two forms: capsules and drops. I find that drops are easier to administer to cats who are often resistant to pills. The pharmacy will tailor the capsule or drop strength according to the instructions of the veterinarian. Initially, it may be prudent to order a three weeks' supply of capsules because the dosage may be adjusted after retesting the animal two weeks into the program.

Veterinarians should specify vegetarian capsules when submitting a prescription. Do not neglect this point. Standard gelatin capsules made from animal protein sources have the potential to cause reactions in sensitive pets. Hydrocortisone is compounded with olive or sesame oil to enhance uptake by fat-sensitive cellular receptor sites for cortisol in the intestines. About 5 percent of my patients are sensitive to the oil or the gelatin capsules. For them, this is not a viable option. I switch them back to the pharmaceutical cortisone. Sensitivity manifests as a return of the original condition. A retest of the hormone levels will show estrogen starting to elevate.

Dealing with Malabsorption

The clinician must always be alert to the presence of malabsorption, particularly when treating an animal with a life-threatening condition. In such situations one cannot afford to assume the patient can absorb an oral medication.

An IgA score below 60 milligrams on the endocrine-immune test indicates probable intestinal inflammation and malabsorption. Until the level rises above 60 milligrams, as determined by a subsequent test, I utilize intramuscular injections to ensure effective delivery of the medication. Once the level rises over 60 milligrams I usually switch patients to oral therapy.

For intramuscular injections I initially use a combination of Vetalog and Depomedrol. Vetalog delivers cortisone into the system immediately, promotes rapid relief, and remains active for about five to seven days. Depomedrol, prepared in a slow-release solution, kicks in around the fifth day. The effects last two to three weeks.

Initial intramuscular (IM) dosages:
- Vetalog: 1 milligram per 10 pounds of body weight.
- Depomedrol: 1 milligram per 1 pound of body weight.
- For critical cases, I often double the quantity of both compounds.

I routinely retest animals after two weeks. The results tell me how to proceed. If the estrogen level is still too high, and the IgA too low, I increase the amount of Depomedrol by 5 to 10 milligrams. After the first injection, I only use the long-acting Depomedrol.

An estrogen level below the normal range indicates a need to reduce the dosage of Depomedrol in any subsequent injection. Estrogen in the normal range suggests staying with the initial Depomedrol dosage.

About 15 percent of the animals I treat require IM injections with Depomedrol for the rest of their lives. After their imbalances normalize, maintenance injections can usually be given at one-month intervals. These particular pets cannot absorb oral synthetic medications and will develop signs of illness. The synthetic medication does not penetrate the mucus membranes of the gut. The options are to use intramuscular injections long term, or try natural cortisone capsules (see below). If a pet owner does not want to go to the expense of having the injections administered at the clinic, we instruct them how to do it themselves.

Once normal levels are attained, I recommend retesting estrogen, T3 and T4, IgA, IgG, and IgM after a month and then after three to six months. If the levels are normal, and clinical signs are gone, then retest yearly.

If asked to treat an animal with a critical case of cancer, autoimmune or feline viral disease, I generally assume the presence of malabsorption. I prefer to keep the patient in the hospital for two to five days.

During that time I administer an intravenous protocol that includes lactated ringers (a combination of sodium and potassium), B complex vitamins, a soluble cortisone preparation, and, if needed, an antibiotic. After five days, the animal is usually switched to the intramuscular protocol until the malabsorption resolves. Then I introduce oral medication. In life-threatening crises, however, you must initially use an IV approach. To do anything else may result in a dead patient.

Cortisone and Fertility

Reproductive problems frequently surface in animals with endocrine-immune imbalances, a result of disturbed immune function and inflammation in the mucous membranes of the uterus or ovaries. Female dogs may experience infertility, false pregnancies, abbreviated estrus ("silent" heat), cystic ovaries, and infections such as pyometra. Cats are also affected, but to a lesser degree.

Veterinarians generally fear that the use of cortisone interferes with fertilization or causes structural defects in the offspring. This may indeed apply to pregnant dogs who do not have a cortisol-based endocrine-immune problem. I have not experienced complications when I correct cortisol defects with low, physiologic dosages of cortisone plus thyroid. To the contrary, subsequent attempts at breeding are usually quite successful. I recall one case of a champion English Bulldog who had aborted three consecutive times in her first trimester. I tested her, found the imbalances, and corrected them. The next time I heard from the owner he reported that the dog had produced ten healthy puppies, all of whom became champions at a young age.

It is interesting to point out that William Jefferies, M.D., an emeritus endocrinologist at the University of Virginia, many years ago reported finding mild deficiencies of cortisol in women with fertility problems. In a 1955 *New England Journal of Medicine* article, Jefferies described correcting the deficiencies and resolving the infertility with small, safe, physiologic dosages of cortisone that could be continued indefinitely. Allergies and rheumatoid arthritis also improved, he reported. I discuss more about Jefferies, a pioneer in the clinical application of cortisone, in Chapter Sixteen.

Important Considerations When Retesting

When you retest for endocrine-immune status after initiating therapy, keep the following points in mind:

- The new cortisol measurement will not reflect the presence of any synthetic cortisone preparations such as Prednisone, Vetalog, or Medrol.
- The score reflects only the level of cortisol in the body, including varying amounts of inactive hormone. But the test will reflect the addition of any natural cortisol replacement used in the program. The natural preparation will change the cortisol score in any retesting.

    The reason for the discrepancy is this: the natural cortisone has a chemical structure identical or close enough to the body's own cortisol so that it, too, becomes measured. Synthetics do not have that close an affinity.

- When you retest an animal taking a synthetic cortisone medication, you want to see the level of cortisol remain the same or even come in at an even lower score than the baseline value. This indicates a good response from the hypothalamic-pituitary feedback system controlling adrenal secretions. The hypothalamus and pituitary sense more cortisol/cortisone in the body. The system reduces the release of ACTH. Less ACTH means less stimulation of the adrenals to produce more cortisol. The use of synthetics in the replacement therapy program will result in a lower cortisol level when you retest endocrine-immune levels. The case histories later in this chapter illustrate this important point.

Replacing Thyroid

I have found it necessary to use only a T4 supplement. When I used a combined T3/T4 supplement in the past I discovered that the net effect was to suppress natural thyroid hormone production. As a result I have not used the combined medication for years.

Today's generics seem to be as reliable, if not better, than the name brands. I use Soloxine, but other forms are available. I suggest .10 (one tenth) of a milligram per 10 pounds of body weight twice a day for both dogs and cats. Most animals respond nicely to this standard dosage. If necessary, the amount can be slowly increased until desired results are obtained.

I have not encountered absorption problems with oral thyroid medication even in the presence of substantial malabsorption.

Thyroid for Dogs

Most dogs need thyroid replacement as part of a successful therapy program. T3/T4 levels may test normal but in fact be bound to some degree because of the influence of cortisol and estrogen abnormalities. If T4 is normal, veterinarians believe that you do not need to supplement. However, there may be an overlooked blockage that dictates otherwise.

To help determine the presence of such blockage, I recommend doing a simple heart rate check. If the animal already takes thyroid medication, test six hours after the time he or she receives the medication when the blood level of thyroid peaks. If not on thyroid, the test can be done anytime.

The pet owner can readily perform this simple heart rate test and report the results. Gently take the left front leg of a standing dog, flex the elbow back onto the left side of the chest, and apply the fingertips in the area where the flexed elbow touches the chest. This is the general location where the ventricular heartbeat can be most easily felt. Count the heart rate for 60 seconds.

A normal range of 95 to 120 heartbeats per minute indicates no blockage. A lower rate indicates blockage, a T4 to T3 transference problem, or a thyroid deficiency, factors that dictate a need to supplement.

Thyroid for Cats

Cats seem to be able to utilize their thyroid output even in the face of cortisol-estrogen interference. Thyroid replacement is indicated when T3 and T4 levels are low, reflecting an obvious hypothyroid condition. Replacement is also needed to treat endocrine-immune defective cats with feline infectious peritonitis.

Case Histories: Interpreting the Whole Animal

The following case histories are meant to enhance the understanding of testing and therapy integration.

Dogs

CASE # 1: IDIOPATHIC EPILEPSY

Patient: Fifty-pound Basset-mixed breed, male, non-neutered, one-year-old.

Clinical signs: *Grand mal* seizures weekly. Each of this dog's five littermates had developed seizures by the age of one.

Baseline E-I One test:

CORTISOL	.27 ug/dl	(significantly low)
ESTROGEN	28.2 pg/ml	(significantly high)
T3	100.2 ng/dl	(low normal)
T4	2.1 ug/dl	(low normal)
IgA	36 mg/dl	(significantly low)
IgG	650 mg/dl	(significantly low)
IgM	72 mg/dl	(significantly low)

Treatment: I prescribed phenobarbital for immediate seizure control. Due to very low IgA level, I suspected malabsorption and started hormone replacement therapy with an intramuscular injection of 5 milligrams of Vetalog combined with 50 milligrams of Depomedrol. I also prescribed Soloxine thyroid medication, at .5 milligram strength, twice daily. The dog was started on a hypoallergenic diet of cottage cheese and potatoes.

Two-week retest:

CORTISOL	.19 ug/dl	The blood test does not measure synthetic cortisone medications present in the body. The significantly low value here represents the body's own inadequate cortisol that is largely defective or excessively bound, and certainly deficient. Replacement therapy with cortisone compensates for the insufficiency and acts as a proxy for cortisol. The medication funds the feedback mechanism to the pituitary, shutting down the abnormal production of estrogen. The high estrogen level decreases.
ESTROGEN	26.2 pg/ml	(moving towards normal)
T3	150 ng/dl	(improved into normal range)
T4	2.6 ug/dl	(improved into normal range)
IgA	58 mg/dl	(improving, but still low)
IgG	900 mg/dl	(improving, but still low)
IgM	86 mg/dl	(improving, but still low)

Treatment: The degree of improvement enabled me to switch the dog to oral Medrol, 4 milligrams daily. After another retest a few weeks later, estrogen, T3/T4, and antibody levels were all normal. I reduced the phenobarbital to half the original dosage for seven days, then to a quarter, and then stopped. In 80 percent of cases, rebalanced animals do not require any antiepileptic drugs.

The dog was fine for about a month, until he ate a piece of chicken and experienced a seizure. It then became apparent that the dog was sensitive to chicken. Afterward, the pet's owner exercised extreme vigilance with the diet. The dog did well on the program and died of natural causes at seventeen. The important lesson here: pets can react severely to any food sensitivity even after imbalances are corrected.

CASE #2: SEVERE ALLERGIC DERMATITIS

Patient: Sixty-two-pound Golden Retriever, female, spayed, three-year-old.

Clinical signs: Severe "hot spots" or areas of moist, inflamed skin with secondary bacterial invasion; major hair loss with no feathers on legs; chronic ear inflammation. A chronic area of dermatitis with thickened skin, hyper-pigmentation, and itchiness present on the top of both front wrists (acral pruritic lick granulomas). Most people think the condition relates to boredom.

Baseline E-I One test:

CORTISOL	.59 ug/dl	(low)
ESTROGEN	36.6 pg/ml	(moderately high)
T3	97 ng/dl	(slightly low)
T4	1.03 ug/dl	(low)
IgA	61 mg/dl	(slightly low)
IgG	975 mg/dl	(slightly low)
IgM	100 mg/dl	(low normal)

Treatment: Oral Medrol 4 milligrams daily. Soloxine thyroid medication, at .6 milligram strength, prescribed twice daily. I also prescribed a hypoallergenic diet of cottage cheese and potatoes.

Two-week retest:

CORTISOL	.31 ug/dl	(reduced level, but desirable)
ESTROGEN	35.2 pg/ml	(almost into normal range)
T3	150 ng/dl	(normal)
T4	2.6 ug/dl	(normal)
IgA	69 mg/dl	(nearly normal)
IgG	1020 mg/dl	(OK)
IgM	125 mg/dl	(OK)

Treatment: I initiated natural hydrocortisone, 40 milligrams daily. Two weeks later, I tested the dog's estrogen level and found a slight increase to 35.6. This indicated an inadequate therapeutic dosage of hydrocortisone. I raised the amount to 50 milligrams. After two weeks, the estrogen and antibody levels tested in the normal range. All clinical signs subsided.

CASE #3: CANCER OF THE SPLEEN (HEMANGIOSARCOMA)

Patient: Fifty-two-pound Basset-mixed breed, male, neutered, eight years old.

Clinical signs: Large tumor of the spleen with accompanying general malaise, weight loss, and low red blood cell count.

Treatment strategy: This blood-borne tumor has the potential to spread to the right atrium of the heart. If it has spread, tumor removal alone may not be successful. Chemotherapy may be indicated. Restoring normal hormone and antibody levels also may not work if metastasis has occurred.

Ultrasound of the right atrium needs to be performed prior to any surgical procedure to determine whether the heart has been affected. If chemotherapy is administered, the hormone and antibody levels must be monitored carefully. Chemo not only slows down the tumor spread but may also damage the hypothalamus, pituitary, adrenal, and thyroid axis.

In the case of this particular dog, ultrasound showed no spread had occurred. I excised the tumor. A biopsy revealed malignant tissue. I took a blood sample for endocrine-immune testing during surgery.

Baseline E-I One test:

CORTISOL	.42 ug/dl	(low)
ESTROGEN	28.1 pg/ml	(very high)
T3	78 ng/dl	(low)
T4	1.25 ug/dl	(low)
IgA	47 mg/dl	(low)
IgG	690 mg/dl	(low)
IgM	82 mg/dl	(low)

Treatment: As expected with cancer cases, endocrine-immune test values revealed imbalances. Once I had the results in hand, I injected the dog intramuscularly with 5 milligrams of Vetalog combined with 50 milligrams of Depomedrol. I prescribed Soloxine thyroid medication, at .5 milligram strength, twice daily, along with a hypoallergenic diet.

Two-week retest:

CORTISOL	.21 ug/dl	(desirably low)
ESTROGEN	25.9 pg/ml	(returning to normal)
T3	130 ng/dl	(normal)
T4	2.89 ug/dl	(normal)
IgA	59 mg/dl	(improving)
IgG	1300 mg/dl	(normal)
IgM	128 mg/dl	(normal)

Treatment: I switched to oral Medrol at 4-milligram strength, and continued with the Soloxine. Two years later, the patient was retested. The results were normal.

Cats

CASE # 1: FELINE IMMUNODEFICIENCY VIRUS (FIV)

Patient: Ten-pound domestic shorthair, female, spayed, three years old.

Clinical signs: The cat had lost three pounds in two previous months. It was anemic, weak, very thin, and experienced hair loss. A red gingival flare was present just above the gum line of the teeth, indicating an IgA deficiency. The cat tested positive for FIV.

Baseline E-I Two (endocrine-immune + CBC + blood chemistry) test:

CBC results indicated red and white cell suppression. Blood chemistry indicated elevated liver enzymes with low blood protein and albumen levels. The cat apparently was not absorbing food well.

CORTISOL	.19 ug/dl	(very low)
ESTROGEN	39 pg/ml	(very high)
T3	118 ng/dl	(normal)
T4	2.1 ug/dl	(low normal)
IgA	29 mg/dl	(very low)
IgG	495 mg/dl	(very low)
IgM	61 mg/dl	(very low)

Treatment: Test results clearly indicated malabsorption and intestinal inflammation. I injected the cat intramuscularly with 2 milligrams of Vetalog combined with 20 milligrams of Depomedrol. In two weeks, the cat had gained a bit of weight and appeared to be feeling better.

Two-week retest:

CORTISOL	.17 ug/dl	(very low, but desirable)
ESTROGEN	36.2 pg/ml	(still high, but moving towards normal)
T3	132 ng/dl	(normal)
T4	2.8 ug/dl	(normal)
IgA	49 mg/dl	(improving, but still low)
IgG	710 mg/dl	(improving, but still low)
IgM	92 mg/dl	(improving, but still slightly low)

As the estrogen dropped, the red and white blood cell counts increased, as did the liver enzymes.

Treatment: Malabsorption was still a concern because of the low IgA level. I decided to do another intramuscular injection, this time increasing the level of Depomedrol to 30 milligrams. A retest after several weeks showed a near normal level of IgA, along with general improving signs of health. This allowed me to switch over to 10 milligrams daily of Prednisone orally for one month. I then switched the cat to 10 milligrams of natural hydrocortisone, its current regimen. After six months, I retested her for FIV. Results were negative. The cat has now been on the program for seven years and is doing fine.

CASE #2: MILIARY DERMATITIS

Patient: Twelve-pound Siamese, male, neutered, five years old.

Clinical signs: Widespread allergic dermatitis. Major hair loss with areas of inflammation, scabs, and bacterial lesions. Hairballs.

Baseline E-I One test:

CORTISOL	.49 ug/dl	(low)
ESTROGEN	27.1 pg/ml	(high)
T3	71 ng/dl	(low)
T4	.98 ug/dl	(low)
IgA	60 mg/dl	(low)
IgG	980 mg/dl	(very slightly low)
IgM	102 mg/dl	(low normal)

Treatment: 10 milligrams of oral Prednisone.

Two-week retest:

CORTISOL	.19 ug/dl	(very low, but desirable)
ESTROGEN	25.3 pg/ml	(slightly above the normal range)
T3	78 ng/dl	(low)
T4	1.05 ug/dl	(low)
IgA	73 mg/dl	(normal)
IgG	1200 mg/dl	(normal)
IgM	140 mg/dl	(normal)

Treatment: The continued low level of thyroid hormones against a rapid normalization of estrogen indicated a hypothyroid condition. About 10 percent of my feline patients have hypothyroidism. I prescribed .1 milligram of Soloxine twice a day. Cortisone continued, as before. Two weeks later, a retest showed estrogen and thyroid levels normal. For more than a decade the cat has enjoyed excellent health on this combined cortisone-thyroid program.

CASE # 3: FELINE URINARY SYNDROME (FUS)

Patient: Eleven-pound Himalayan, male, neutered, three years old.

Clinical signs: History of two previous urinary tract obstructions. Another veterinarian had suggested post-pubic urethrostomy. Urine pH was alkaline even though the cat had been on a low-ash, low-magnesium, urinary-acidifying diet!

Baseline E-I One test:

CORTISOL	.57 ug/dl	(low)
ESTROGEN	26.8 pg/ml	(high)
T3	121 ng/dl	(normal)
T4	2.6 ug/dl	(normal)
IgA	41 mg/dl	(low)
IgG	787 mg/dl	(low)
IgM	83 mg/dl	(low)

Treatment: Because of the low IgA level, I injected the cat intramuscularly with 2 milligrams of Vetalog and 20 milligrams of Depomedrol. I prescribed digestive enzymes to help breakdown carbohydrates and protein.

Two-week retest:

CORTISOL	.42 ug/dl	(low, but desirable)
ESTROGEN	25.3 pg/ml	(slightly above the normal range)
T3	138 ng/dl	(normal)
T4	2.89 ug/dl	(normal)
IgA	67 mg/dl	(slightly low)
IgG	1095 mg/dl	(normal)
IgM	102 mg/dl	(low normal)

Urine pH was now acidic, due to the digestive enzymes effectively aiding in the breakdown of protein. Improved protein utilization contributes to an acidic pH.

Treatment: The cat continued on 10 milligrams of natural hydrocortisone along with plant-based digestive enzymes. The cat has been fine without any urinary tract problems for ten years.

Troubleshooting

PROBLEM: You have done the blood test and the appropriate hormone replacement. Two weeks later the animal comes in for the follow-up blood test. However, the patient has not improved and is still in poor health.

SOLUTION: If the values are normal, and the pet still shows continuing signs of illness, the likely explanation is food intolerance. That is the only problem you cannot correct with this therapy. You must immediately initiate a remedial dietary program. I cover such a diet in Chapter Ten.

Diet is the outstanding variable. If the hormones are normal, and the patient does not improve, always consider a food sensitivity problem. If the original condition comes and goes, the issue still relates to food. The cause of the problem could even be a snack.

PROBLEM: The patient has received IM medication. A previously high estrogen level has been brought down to the normal range. Oral medication has now been initiated. After two weeks, the animal returns with clinical signs of illness, or excess scratching, once again. The estrogen level is still normal.

SOLUTION: Here is another situation where the patient has a food intolerance interfering with the therapy. The pet must be placed on a hypoallergenic diet. Refer to the next chapter for details.

PROBLEM: The veterinarian increases the intramuscular dosage of cortisone because of lack of improvement. Yet, the increase does not help. There is still no improvement.

SOLUTION: The injection may have inadvertently been administered to subcutaneous tissue, not the muscle, and thus there is no carriage to the blood system. If the test levels are normal in the patient, the problem relates to food sensitivity. The food sensitivity issue must be dealt with as part of this remedial program, otherwise normalization will not occur.

PROBLEM: Within the first three days after the initial injection of cortisone the patient develops side effects such as excess thirst and urination, vomiting, diarrhea, or lethargy.

SOLUTION: These reactions are fairly rare, occurring in perhaps 3 percent to 5 percent of cases. Generally they are mild and last for no longer than twenty-four to forty-eight hours. The problem is usually Vetalog, the short-acting steroid in the injection. You need to replace it and not use it again when you re-inject. This is important. Replace the Vetalog and re-inject with another short-acting steroid such as Prednisone or Prednisolone.

It is possible for Prednisone or Prednisolone to also generate similar side effects. If this occurs, then basically none of the short-acting steroids should be used. You may be able to utilize only Depomedrol, the long-acting steroid. At this stage, Depomedrol is fine because the cortisol defect will by now have been sufficiently corrected. You are no longer dealing with a beginning patient and extreme levels.

The long-term steroid can actually be used alone, and at the same dosage, even in the beginning. However, I mix the two types of cortisone initially in order to obtain a faster normalization.

PROBLEM: Do all acutely critical cases need an IV for the program to succeed?

SOLUTION: I use an IV to make sure the patient survives. I take blood immediately for the endocrine-immune test. Once an animal is stable and comfortable, I consider using oral medication. By then I have done my measurements and I know what I have corrected and controlled. If I use oral cortisone, I monitor the patient carefully. Within a week or two, I recheck the levels. I am very attentive to a possible malabsorption problem.

– TEN –

The Diet Replacement Program

The success of the endocrine-immune program depends on a good partnership between veterinarians and pet owners. In the previous two chapters I lay out the details for testing and administering medication. These are responsibilities of the veterinarian. Once your pet is back at home, you have to do your part. That means administering medication as directed and carefully following a dietary program in support of the therapy. In short, a hypoallergenic diet is essential to the success of the program.

By hypoallergenic diet I mean food that a particular animal can tolerate. If a cat or dog eats an offending food, he or she may have a serious setback or start redeveloping signs of the original condition. An offending food can easily nullify improvement achieved by the endocrine-immune program even though the program is correcting the underlying imbalances. Food is the sole variable that can sabotage the program. For pets with the hormonal-immune defect, food often tends to be a problem, and can be potentially deadly.

Unsure whether your animal has a sensitivity to a particular food? The following procedure can give you a quick, simple answer.

- Immediately after doing the initial endocrine-immune blood test your veterinarian administers an intramuscular injection of Vetalog (1 milligram per 10 pounds of body weight) to your pet.
- Observe the animal for a few days.
- No improvement in health indicates sensitivity to some food or ingredient in the regular diet. The quick-acting cortisone injection usually blocks all allergic reactions except those to food.

I recommend this simple procedure at the time of doing one of the E-I tests because of the critical importance of monitoring food intake for affected animals, and controlling their diet as soon as possible. Food-related sensitivities usually occur only in the presence of hormonal imbalances.

Once a pet develops sensitivity to a specific food or ingredient the immune cells retain the memory of that particular offender. Whenever the pet eats offensive foods the system treats them as antigens, substances that can stimulate an unwanted immune response.

Some people believe they can purge the diet of antigenic foods, or eat less of them, over several weeks and thus eliminate or minimize the sensitivity. This has not been my experience for the past thirty years in dealing with food intolerances. Immune cells remember, and they will react. Even if you have "cleansed" the system, if a pet eats offending foods or ingredients again, the alarm will sound—and even louder than before.

Caregivers need to be diligent—and always honest—when giving a medical and dietary history to the veterinarian. Many times pet owners have given me less than honest answers or overlooked important food-related information as I tried to figure out why the therapy was not working. Sometimes I discovered that their children, unaware of the problem and consequences, were giving offending foods to the family pets.

In frustration I have frequently asked for permission to keep animals at my hospital for a few days at no cost to the pet owner. I put the animals on special diets and inevitably the hormone therapy starts working again. The patients improve. Then I know for sure there is something in the food at home that is setting off the alarm.

The most unusual case I encountered involved a Cairn Terrier named Ardsley who was extremely intolerant to many foods. From time to time, she would eat something offensive and develop diarrhea and vomiting. The owner would bring Ardsley to the clinic and I would find signs of a severe pancreatic reaction. For two years I could not get to the bottom of the problem, even though a hormone replacement program was correcting the dog's endocrine-immune imbalances. Finally, we figured it out. The client's house was close to a Kentucky Fried Chicken restaurant. Ravens and crows were picking up bits of leftover chicken meat and bones from the parking lot and dumpster. Then, on occasion, they would land in my client's yard and leave a bone or small piece of chicken behind. That occasional morsel was enough to alter a supersensitive, highly inbred animal. It was unbelievable!

When Ardsley ate the wrong food, the consequences were potentially lethal. She would quickly develop pancreatitis, an inflammation of the pancreas. One Halloween evening, the dog got into a stash of candy intended for trick-or-treaters. She reacted violently and had to be rushed to an emergency clinic. The owner called me the next morning to report that Ardsley had died.

Obviously, death from food intake is not an everyday situation, but I mention it here to emphasize a real danger for food-sensitive pets. From my observations, severe reactions among these animals have become increasingly frequent.

People have often told me, after questioning, that yes, they gave their animals a snack or a "little bit of this or that now and then." I can assure you that for animals like Ardsley "a little bit of this or that now and then" can set back the therapy, generate a seizure, or even kill.

The Hypoallergenic Diet

The lamb-and-rice hypoallergenic diet I originally created in the early 1980s has been so widely copied that it seems as if every pet food company now markets a lamb and rice product. While intended primarily for dogs, formulations target cats as well. The main consumers, however, are dogs.

This proliferation caused many dogs with endocrine-immune imbalances to become reactive to lamb and rice. It is a case of too much exposure, eating the same food over and over. This development prompted me to come up with another hypoallergenic concept—"Innovative Veterinary Diets"—formulated in the late 1980s for Nature's Recipe, available on prescription from veterinarians. Other companies market products similar to IVD, and are sold also through veterinarians or at pet stores.

I recommend these types of products to clients who put their animals on my endocrine-immune program, particularly during the critical initial period of the therapy. These recipes represent a simple and convenient way around the food challenge. They contain just two ingredients—a protein and a carbohydrate source—in order to minimize the possibility of reactions. The protein is derived from duck, venison, fish, and rabbit.

The products for dogs contain potatoes as the source of carbohydrate. The reason for the use of potatoes, and not rice, is because many canines have developed intolerance to rice due to excessive exposure to lamb and rice diets.

Originally, my formula for cats was the same as for dogs: meat combined with potatoes. Following the purchase of Nature's Recipe by H. J. Heinz Company in 1996, the company switched the carbohydrate source from potatoes to peas, a result of testing that showed peas to be more palatable. However, many cats cannot tolerate peas and develop diarrhea and vomiting. To avoid this potential problem do not use the IVD cat products. Use the dog recipes with potatoes instead. They work fine. If you do switch, be sure to supplement your cat daily with 800 milligrams of taurine, an essential amino acid for felines. A taurine deficiency may cause cardiomyopathy, an enlargement of the heart.

If you continue with a hypoallergenic product like this, rotate meats every four months or so in order to help prevent intolerances from developing. Thus, you might feed duck and potatoes for four months, then rabbit and potatoes.

Rotation-type diets are available in canned and kibble forms. The main difference: dry kibble contains very little moisture and is far more concentrated than the canned food. Moreover, the kibble contains three times more carbohydrates than the canned and is thus three times more fattening. Some people prefer kibble because of the economy factor. It takes less kibble to feed and satisfy a dog than canned food. A half-and-half combination of canned and kibble may be a practical compromise. For an overweight dog, feed canned food until the weight comes down. For a thin dog, feed kibble to bump the weight up.

If an animal is intolerant to chicken, there may be a similar intolerance to other fowl such as duck. So be alert to that possibility. If you encounter a reaction to any IVD-type product, try the following strategy:

- For seven days feed your pet only cottage cheese and rice.
- Then add boiled white potatoes for another seven days. If a reaction occurs, then the entire line of protein with potatoes is a no-no. If there is no problem with the potatoes, then switch to a product with a different protein source.

Keep in mind that all hypoallergenic products are not created equal. One product from Manufacturer A may be well tolerated by your pet, but the same food combination from Manufacturer B is not well tolerated. This includes IVD products, which some animals will not like or tolerate. The explanation is simple: one product has something in it that does not agree with your pet.

I use IVD products in my practice and generally have good results with them. However, I am no longer involved in their formulation and cannot guarantee that IVD, or any other manufactured food for that matter, will be tolerated by a particular pet. Each animal is individual. Products, and even batches within product lines, are also individual and subject to ingredient or quality changes. Go with what works. Always be alert to possible reactions.

Usually, a sick pet improves substantially during the initial few weeks of therapy as long as the pet does not eat an offending food. Once any malabsorption problem has been cleared up, hormonal replacement dosages are adjusted based on follow-up blood tests, and soon the pet is on a routine maintenance schedule. You can then opt to continue with the special food or carefully start introducing other foods into the diet that may be more economical. If you do the latter, I suggest following a simple add-back plan that I designed for my clients.

The Add-Back Plan

Start with a limited diet of cottage cheese and potatoes, or add cottage cheese to the special hypoallergenic food product your pet already eats. Cottage cheese works fine for most animals. Do this for a week. During this time check the stools. You want to see well-formed feces with no evidence of mucous or blood. If there are no signs of food intolerance such as itching, scratching, stomach upset or diarrhea, then continue with a slow add back of foods, one at a time, and preferably none of the items on the "HIT Lists." (See Chapter Six.)

Use home-cooked foods first, perhaps some vegetables and chicken. If there are no reactions, you might find a commercial chicken product for pets and test it the same way the following week. Make sure the contents are free of common offenders or chemicals. See if your animal does as well as on the home-cooked chicken.

You can continue to add back any single food item to the regular diet after it has passed the seven-day test. You can then rotate and mix within the boundaries of tolerated food. In this way, you can soon develop an individualized hypoallergenic menu for your pet. But remember—you add back only one food per week.

Every four to six months change the diet a bit in order to prevent a sensitivity developing due to constant exposure to the same food. Change the protein and the carbohydrate sources. You may go from potatoes to rice, or from chicken to beef.

Years ago I found many dogs intolerant to beef because they were eating it endlessly day after day. With the advent of the lamb and rice diets people then stopped the beef and began feeding lamb and rice. And after feeding this on a daily basis for years, pets then began developing intolerance to the once hypoallergenic lamb and rice. Today, many pets have not been exposed much to beef. Thus, beef may no longer be the problem it once was. You can always re-introduce beef and see how it goes. In any case, always rotate the food—both protein and carbohydrate sources—every four to six months.

Other tips for dealing with food sensitivities:

- Do not include any chew sticks, vitamins, dog biscuits, or snacks when you are food testing. Any one of these items could cause reactions. All foods and even nutritional supplements are guilty until proven innocent.
- Always be wary of snacks. Test anything you give your animal to eat. Test it for seven days to make sure there are no adverse reactions.
- It is OK to feed from the table if you yourself eat a healthy diet. Unseasoned pastas, vegetables, and salad can be mixed into a base diet. But if your animal starts to scratch, vomit, has diarrhea, or becomes lethargic, than take heed. You may have fed something that your animal companion cannot tolerate. Use common sense.
- Standard (non-hypoallergenic) kibble, while offering great feeding convenience and economy, represents a potentially major source of food reactivity problems. Inside those chunks and nuggets are multiple ingredients, including some that may cause problems for sensitive pets. Kibble contains little moisture and the ingredients are highly concentrated, meaning potentially more allergenic.
- Stay away from the cheap plain-wrap generic pet food products sold widely throughout the United States and Canada. They likely contain questionable ingredients and are often reject or substandard chows sold out the "back door" by major manufacturers. In addition,

avoid high-protein kibble. Your pet does not need extra amounts of poor-quality protein.

- When considering any commercial pet food, always read the ingredient label. The shorter the ingredient list the better. The longer the list, the worse the diet. The first three ingredients on the label usually make up 90 percent of the contents.

- Avoid products with chemical additives on the label. These substances include BHA, BHT, and ethoxyquin, preservatives, stabilizers, artificial colors, flavors, and sweeteners. Realistically you can never be sure if they are in the food, even if they are not listed on the label. Nor can you know if residues of drugs, hormones, and antibiotics used to fatten feed animals have survived through the manufacturing process and are present in the food. Your only recourse is to stop feeding any food you suspect is making your pet ill. Cheap prices usually mean poor ingredients. But even while price may reflect quality, you can still have a pricey food that may have some questionable ingredients.

  Chemical additives have the potential to create toxic effects over time and perhaps even damage the adrenal cortex, where cortisol is produced. The cortex is the major target for toxicity in the endocrine system. Such toxicity might lead to temporary or even permanent endocrine-immune imbalances in a normal pet. In a pet who already has imbalances such chemicals have the potential to cause catastrophic effects.

- Fresh and wholesome foods are, of course, much better for pets just as they are for humans. If you can feed organic foods you can reduce the burden of unwanted chemicals. But even good quality foods have the potential to cause reactions in sensitive animals with hormonal-immune imbalances. This includes raw meat. The food may be great, but your pet just may not be able to tolerate it. That goes for vegetables as well. Even though they may be healthy and natural, your particular pet may not tolerate some of them. Remember the individuality of each pet.

Raw or Cooked? The Meat Controversy

The issue of raw food, and particularly raw meat, is a controversial one among veterinarians and knowledgeable breeders. I believe in raw foods, particularly fruits and vegetables that are high in various important nutrients, which are destroyed in the cooking process. However, I have been against raw meat of any kind for many years. There is too high a risk for bacterial contamination.

Dogs and cats, of course, evolved on raw meat. Many veterinarians, particularly in the alternative medicine field, recommend raw meat in order to create and sustain good health. They often say this type of food has the potential to clear up many health problems for a large majority of pets. I have no doubt about the sincerity and observations of these professionals who believe that most pets have the enzymes and immune resources to destroy the routine food-borne microorganisms. However, the vast majority of my patients have compromised endocrine-immune systems. I fear that they do not have the resources to wage an effective defense when exposed to harmful bacteria such as Salmonella or E. coli present in raw meat. The bacteria could spread rapidly and put an animal into crisis.

Over the years I have treated some severely imbalanced dogs and cats whose owners insisted on feeding them raw meat. Their pets then developed horrific intestinal upset, pancreatitis, bacteria in the bloodstream, and a crisis situation where antibiotics had to be used immediately and many times were ineffective.

I have carefully weighed the merits of raw meat versus cooked meats. I conclude that for my patients, cooked meat represents less of a chance to develop a catastrophic bacterial disease than raw meat.

Jim Simpson, D.V.M., an Oregon veterinarian who has been using my program for years, recalls the case of Spice, a Golden Retriever who developed skin problems, bloody diarrhea, and vomiting. The couple who owned the dog disagreed on the raw meat issue. The wife strongly believed in raw meat and bones, but the pet had severe hormonal-immune imbalances and could not handle raw meat.

"I started Spice on the hormone replacement program and a hypoallergenic diet and all went well," says Dr. Simpson. "All the clinical signs of illness disappeared. Retesting showed all the endocrine-immune values in the normal range. The owners followed the program and administered the medication as I prescribed."

About a year later, the dog got sick again with all the signs of the previous illness. The couple brought Spice back to Dr. Simpson's clinic. When he questioned them, the wife assured the vet that they had been loyal to the program and were not doing anything different. The husband, however, appeared to be furious.

"I thought he was angry with me because somehow the program

was not working," recalls Dr. Simpson. "So I said to him, 'It looks like you want to tell me something, so you might as well get it off your chest.' To my surprise, he angrily turned to his wife, and in a loud voice, said, 'Tell him the damn truth! You have been feeding the raw diet again. Be honest with this man.'"

At that point, she admitted she had indeed started feeding raw meat again. Dr. Simpson told her that her dog could not really handle that kind of a diet, no matter how good she thought it was. And the fact was, even though a lot of people swear by a raw food diet, she was hurting her dog by insisting on it.

"I thought the information had sunk in, but six months later she started again," Dr. Simpson says. "And Spice got sick all over again." This time she said she had learned her lesson. It has now been about five years and Spice has been doing great. No more recurrences.

"I've had several other cases like this. For some people feeding raw is almost a religion," observes Dr. Simpson. "And some animals just can not handle it, and they suffer as a result."

In my practice I have encountered this kind of situation quite a few times. The pet goes on the therapy program, improves substantially, and then suddenly becomes ill again because the pet owner insists on feeding certain foods. Raw meat may be natural from an evolutionary perspective, but natural or not, it may hurt many of today's domesticated and very unnatural pets.

There is another important point to consider: many pets are intolerant to specific kinds of meat—chicken or beef or lamb, for example—whether cooked or raw. Thus, the problem could be that the meat is raw, or the problem could be the meat itself.

This brings up the subject of bones. Many people regularly feed bones to their pets believing that bones help clean the teeth as animals gnaw on them. Indeed bones may clean the biting surfaces of the teeth but there are risks involved, such as perforating the stomach and intestinal linings when they ingest bone slivers. Moreover, a pet could be allergic to the meat on the bone or become infected from bacterial contamination if the bone is raw. I never recommend bones, raw or cook, big or small. I have treated too many animals suffering from vomiting, diarrhea or bloody stools because of bones.

— ELEVEN —

Supplements and Natural Remedies

Boss was a superdog in every way—the star of the Beverly Hills Police Department's Canine Corps for years. The highly trained German Shepherd helped apprehend dozens of criminals. In 1982 he captured top honors as the best police dog in California by winning the "Police Dog Olympics," a competition involving obedience tests, obstacle courses, speed drills, and attack skills.

Within a year, however, Boss developed periodic lameness in the legs. During vigorous activity he would abruptly stop, pull up lame, and go down in obvious agony. This could occur after jumping a barrier during a training session or chasing a ball in the backyard. He would be laid up and lame for four to six weeks after each episode.

As the problem continued, Officer Jay Broyles, the dog's handler, brought him in to see me in 1984. "Luckily, there has been no problem on the job," Broyles said. "Boss has always performed marvelously. Once he saved my life by attacking an armed suspect who would otherwise have shot me. But there has been a nagging fear in the back of my mind that something could happen at a critical moment. I'm very attached to the dog and very concerned about losing him."

Broyles had previously consulted with another veterinarian who diagnosed pan-osteitis, a bone disease that strikes puppies. The diagnosis was puzzling to me because the dog was already three years old and pan-osteitis is extremely rare in adult dogs.

I examined Boss and found a chronic skin disorder on his back, underside, and heels. A test for endocrine-immune imbalances revealed a typical pattern of disorder. A stool sample to check out his trypsin level showed a shortage in this important digestive enzyme produced by the pancreas. (See more on trypsin in the next section on malabsorption.) The combination of problems was causing severe malabsorption, which seriously affected Boss's nutrient intake, including calcium and other minerals vital for bone integrity. The dog's bones were not properly mineralized and that was causing pain and lameness.

I recommended cortisol replacement therapy and supplementation with enzymes and trace minerals. At my behest, Broyles eliminated the commercial brand of dry food he was feeding to Boss and started him on a hypoallergenic diet. I thought this might help with what appeared to be a typical food-related skin allergy.

Boss responded dramatically to the program. In less than two months he appeared to be his old stalwart self again. The skin disorder cleared up quickly, and his hair coat became radiant. Broyles reported that Boss added more muscle and was more alert than ever. Most importantly, the pain and lameness never recurred.

Boss improved to such a degree that he was entered in the 1985 "Police Dog Olympics." He had not competed since 1982 because of his condition. Afterward, an elated Broyles called to tell me that Boss outperformed the cream of California's canine cops—forty-nine other highly trained dogs—to win another gold medal. A few months later, he took top honors at the first-ever "Police and Fire World Olympics." Boss stayed healthy on the program over many years and lived to be about fourteen years old.

Malabsorption and Enzyme Replacement

Malabsorption, the inability to properly absorb nutrients from food, is a major problem that veterinarians do not discuss much. I find that about 70 percent of my patients cannot digest food properly. The problem is frequently due to the endocrine-immune defect that causes a destabilization of IgA in the gut, leading to subsequent inflammation in the intestinal lining.

But often a lack of adequate digestive enzymes can be the culprit, and specifically a deficiency of trypsin. Trypsin is a major pancreatic digestive enzyme that contributes to the breakdown of protein, fats, and carbohydrates. The classic sign of a deficiency is an animal eating its own stool.

In my practice I routinely test animals for trypsin. Over the years I have determined that nearly a quarter of them—dogs and cats alike—have mild to moderate deficiencies. When animals cannot extract enough nutrition from food they will often turn to stool eating. Dogs love cat stool, for instance, because protein levels are excessively high in canned or dry cat food and cats cannot totally digest the food. The undigested protein passes into the stool. Dogs sniff it out, find it of interest, and eat it.

The impact of deficiency may show up early in kittens and puppies as soon as they start eating solid food. They may grow at a slower pace or not reach full size. The signs could also possibly take several years to develop. Often there is an allergic-like dermatitis, hair loss, and red, scaly, itchy skin that animals constantly gnaw on. You may see large stools with undigested fat clearly visible. In some rapidly growing puppies, hunting and working dogs, the malabsorption may cause a weakness and lameness.

The causes of enzyme deficiency are basically two-fold:

- Genetic. Years ago I traced deficiencies through generations of Abyssinian and Persian cats, and through generations of German Shepherds, Dobermans, and Irish Setters. This was a case of one generation passing it along to another. However, today I find deficiencies in virtually all purebreeds and mixed breeds. For me this represents yet another example of fallout from hormonal-immune imbalances generated by contemporary breeding practices. The imbalances cause a systemic loss of lymphocyte and antibody function, and if the pancreas is affected, the production of important enzymes may be compromised. The pancreas makes an array of digestive enzymes as well as insulin, the hormone that controls the level of blood sugar. Thus suppression of normal pancreas activity can result in a trypsin deficiency and perhaps allow for the development of diabetes.
- Acquired. Viral and bacterial infection, or any insult to the pancreas, can negatively affect trypsin production. The aging process also slows down the pancreas and often interferes with enzyme activity. Digestive enzymes are frequently deficient in older or sickly animals.

The solution for the enzyme problem can often be fairly simple—the addition of a quality pet digestive enzyme supplement mixed directly into the food. I always recommend digestive enzymes for common skin problems. The supplements provide missing enzymes that help break down food and facilitate the absorption of essential nutrients. By improving absorption, the supplements benefit the entire system, including the skin.

I only recommend pet digestive enzyme supplements derived from plant sources and never supplements made from bovine or porcine sources because pets may be intolerant to beef and pork. Moreover, if the enzymes are extracted from aging cows and pigs, the supplements may not contain enough enzymatic firepower to do the job. Plant-based enzymes are also less expensive.

When you purchase these supplements you will notice that they contain protease, amylase, and lipase. These are pancreatic enzymes that break down protein, carbohydrates, and fats respectively. You will not see trypsin on the label simply because trypsin is too expensive to utilize in supplement form. The other pancreatic enzymes used in supplement formulations do the job of aiding digestion quite effectively.

If your veterinarian does a stool test for trypsin and the results are normal there could still be a problem. This is because the animal's production of trypsin may be simply overwhelmed by the concentration of nutrients present in many of the contemporary pet diets, particularly kibble. The result is malabsorption of food and often intolerance to food. So, in essence, a type of deficiency may exist even if the test comes back normal. The pancreas can only produce a certain amount of enzymes. This is a frequently overlooked point.

Another point to consider is that a hormonally imbalanced pet eating a poor-quality diet could possibly develop inflammation and irritation in the gut leading to a loss of absorption of nutrients. Switching to a better quality diet, whether pet food or human-grade food, might correct malabsorption if the original poor diet had caused the malabsorption.

Many veterinarians associate an enzyme deficiency with pets who are thin yet have a ravenous appetite. I have encountered many cases, however, where the deficiency has contributed to obesity. This often occurs as a consequence of concentrated kibble formulations that are simply too concentrated. Animals cannot readily digest all that they eat. Compared to protein and fats, carbohydrates are the most abundant food constituent in these commercial products, and the most easily broken down by the body and assimilated. The carbohydrate excess contributes to obesity, whether an enzyme deficiency exists or not. An inability to properly digest proteins and fats also can lead to a habit called "pica," where animals eat inanimate objects.

Pica is an overlooked aspect of malabsorption. You would be surprised at some of the things animals consume: plastic, socks, panty hose, thread, string, and paper, just to name a few. In addition to the concentrated composition of diets, pica can also be caused by an enzyme deficiency that prevents animals from absorbing their nutritional needs, food that is lacking in adequate mineral content, and food intolerances that aggravate the intestines and interfere with normal absorption.

Several years ago I treated two Golden Retriever brothers who had pica. The dogs were both two years old. One was all skin and bones and the other was obese. Testing indicated that both had normal production of enzymes. However, further investigation revealed that the thin dog could not break down protein, carbohydrates, or fat very well because of the richness of the diet. His much heavier brother could process carbohydrate, but had trouble with protein and fats. I put both dogs on a digestive enzyme supplement to help them digest their food. Both improved dramatically and their weights normalized.

Nutritional Supplements

Over the years I have routinely recommended supplementation. However, due to modern-day endocrine-immune imbalances in animals, initially I do not know if a supplement will be helpful or detrimental to a pet's health. Once I determine that the endocrine-immune imbalance is controlled, then supplements can be tried. I tell my clients that if finances are a concern, it is more important to be sure your pet's endocrine-immune system is in balance by getting the blood test. Also, a healthy, nonallergenic diet is essential and will often contain many of the needed vitamins and minerals.

There are major minerals such as calcium, magnesium, potassium, and zinc that are important for health along with dozens of other lesser-known, trace elements. Because the soil we grow our food in is often deficient in minerals, supplements can be beneficial. In many thousands of cases I have found that trace minerals help in many ways. Within a six-month period, I usually see the following kind of results:

- Improvement in general health;
- Darker, thicker hair coat with increased luster;
- Reduced scratching;
- Reduced flakiness;
- Better maintenance of body weight with reduced caloric intake;
- In geriatric cats and dogs, increased activity, and improved condition of hair coat;

■ Animals plagued by fleas usually appear to improve within a few weeks, and attract far fewer fleas.

Over the years dry, itchy, scaly skin has often been treated with omega-3 fatty acid supplements. A deficiency of fatty acids is fairly common. Supplementation can make a big difference in the health of the skin and hair coat. My preference in supplements has been special fish oil-based omega-3 products that are contaminant free.

How to Add Supplements

If you are following the endocrine-immune therapy program, wait for at least a few weeks before starting supplements. Give the therapy a chance to work on its own. You want to be sure the therapy program and the supportive diet have been fine-tuned before adding another element into the equation.

Wait until your pet has been retested, usually after two weeks into the program, and you have seen improvement. By this time you and your veterinarian will be familiar with the hormone replacement procedure and the diet. You can then introduce supplements for added benefits and optimum nutrition.

You must monitor the supplements carefully. Pets may react to one or more ingredients in a supplement formula just as they might to some ingredients in the diet. Go slow, as you do introducing new food. Administer the supplement at the time you feed your pet and for the first week at half the dosage. Some supplements are in capsule or tablet form, others are available as powder that can be sprinkled onto food. Add one supplement at a time, watching for any adverse reactions. If your pet does not have a problem with the supplement over the period of a week that indicates the particular formula is being tolerated and you can then use the recommended full dosage. Then add another supplement, if you choose, and also put it to the one-week test. I suggest adding supplements in the following sequence:

1) Enzymes, plant-based digestive enzymes
2) Multiple vitamin, plant-based only
3) Other supplements, such as a fatty acid

If a pet reacts to a supplement, you will probably see the same kind of reactions as with food intolerance. You might see a return of the original clinical signs that had been improved by the therapy, or perhaps scratching, loose stools, diarrhea, vomiting, or blood in the urine.

How would you know whether the food or the supplement is causing problems? Always start the add-back program first with the food. Wait to start the supplements after you have worked out a trouble-free diet.

Over the years, many new clients have told me they give supplements and natural remedies to their pets but do not see any apparent benefits. The reason for this is that even the best of supplements and natural remedies may not work in the presence of endocrine-immune imbalances. There may be an inability to absorb supplements because of an enzyme deficiency, a food sensitivity, or malabsorption in the gut. You need to test for imbalances or deficiencies, and if they exist, correct those first. Then consider the option of supplements.

Recommendations

▪ **Enzymes**

Dr. Goodpet's Canine Digestive Enzymes or Feline Digestive Enzymes. Species-specific powdered formulas made from plant-based sources of digestive enzymes. Available in health food stores, pet stores, or through Dr. Goodpet, Inglewood, CA, (800) 222-9932 or the company's website: www.goodpet.com.

Terra Oceana's Enzyme Plus. A natural organic powder formulation of plant-based enzymes. Available through Terra Oceana Inc., Montecito, CA, at (800) 989-6929 (orders only) or (805) 640-9429, or from the company's website: www.terraoceana.com. Their products are for humans and animals.

Rainbow Light's AllZyme Double Strength. Plant-based enzymes in capsule form. Available in health food stores. Contact Rainbow Light, Santa Cruz, CA, (800) 635-1233, or through the company's website: www.rainbowlight.com. Their products are for humans and animals.

▪ **Daily Multivitamin and Mineral Supplements**

Terra Oceana's Power for Life. This plant-based powdered formula is packed with green, organic superfoods providing vitamins, minerals, antioxidants, herbs, and phytonutrients, for humans and animals.

Rainbow Light's Master Nutrient Systems. The nutrients in this supplement are added to a base of whole foods and herbs.

Rainbow Light's Advanced Mineral System. This iron-free mineral formula may be used as a trace mineral supplement designed to aid digestion and absorption.

Rainbow Light's Calcium "+." Each tablet provides 166 milligrams of calcium and 333 milligrams of magnesium to aid in the prevention of heart problems.

- **Pharmaceutical-grade fish oil supplements**
  These purified supplements can help animals with dry skin and other common external problems. Fish oils are rich in omega-3 essential fatty acids, and act as anti-inflammatory agents and precursors in the body for hormone production. They also help protect against coronary artery occlusion. This product is for humans and animals. Pharmaceutical-grade means the supplements are free of mercury and DDT.

  Omega Rx. From Sears Laboratories, Marblehead, MA. Phone: (800) 404-8171.

  SAM-EPA. From Biotech, Fayetteville, AR. Phone: (800) 345-1199.

  For either one of these products, I recommend 1 capsule once a day for animals up to 40 pounds, and 2 capsules once a day for larger dogs.

- **Miscellaneous Supplements**
  Terra Oceana's Probiotics Plus. An organic proprietary blend of probiotic and friendly soil-based bacteria, in powder form, designed to protect and restore digestive and intestinal integrity and also support immunity.

  Coenzyme Q10. CoQ10 is a powerful antioxidant supplement that energizes the body, aids the heart, and also helps prevent gum disease. It is particularly beneficial for pets with heart and periodontal disease. Administer any quality CoQ10 product along with meals for best effect. Pets up to 40 pounds take one 30-milligram capsule daily. Over 40 pounds, use one capsule twice a day.

— TWELVE —

Dogs in Balance

In this chapter I have selected a number of canine cases from my clinical work to share in the hope that they will inspire interest in the potential of endocrine-immune therapy. Keep in mind that while I am showcasing single conditions here, patients often have multiple problems. The hormonal replacement program cannot mend each and every problem, but it heals a broad range of conditions that veterinarians often have difficulty treating.

Aggressive Brothers

One of my long-standing clients had two Golden Retriever littermates I treated for chronic skin allergies. The animals were maintained for years on a hormonal program and lived to be about fifteen. After they died the owner wanted two more like them, so she contacted the breeder in Oregon who had some of the frozen sperm from the father. The inseminated female produced a litter and my client bought two male puppies.

The pups were beautiful, spirited dogs and did not show any problems until eleven months of age. At that time they got into a vicious fight and almost killed each other. They inflicted multiple wounds on each other that required extensive sutures.

I tested the dogs and found a cortisol deficiency and high estrogen. I put both on a hormone replacement program and the dogs were fine—for awhile. A trainer unfamiliar with my program questioned the cortisone therapy. He influenced the owner to stop the medication "because it would damage the dogs' health." He made other recommendations, such as to avoid feeding them together. So the owner started cutting down the cortisone and soon stopped the program altogether. The dogs then got into another battle royal.

The owner, visibly shaken and feeling contrite, returned to my clinic with the dogs, both with multiple and bloody bite wounds. We started the program once again. The dogs have been good pals, eating and playing together, without problems for three years.

Separation Anxiety

Billy became agitated whenever his owner left for work. This intact nine-month-old bull-mastiff chewed up furniture and everything in sight, so the owner locked him in the bathroom. Billy proceeded to chew the door.

Another veterinarian prescribed Clomicalm, a sedative that is often used for these problems. The medication did not help. The owner came to me for another opinion. I tested the dog and found typical low cortisol and high estrogen values. I started Billy on hormonal replacement therapy and left him on the Clomicalm for two weeks. As his hormonal imbalances straightened out, I weaned him off the sedative.

The dog mellowed out quickly. He has been on the program for more than four years and has been a model of calmness ever since. No more anxiety separation.

In cases like this, where the imbalances impact the emotions of a pet, remedial training and behavioral therapy may not work until the underlying hormonal disturbances are corrected. Some dogs with these common problems are euthanized because they cannot be handled.

Abnormal Sexual Behavior

Over the years I have had many new clients ask me why their female dogs are mounting other females. This is an expression of the imbalance. Malfunction in the adrenal cortex has led to not only an elevated level of estrogen but also testosterone as well. Some female dogs will then behave like males. Addressing the cortisol deficiency stops the ACTH stimulation, and the extra estrogen and testosterone production.

Ruth, a three-year-old spayed Golden Retriever, was a prime example. At eighteen months of age she started mounting a teddy bear in the house as well as her owners' legs. First, the dog was spayed. Then, in order to break the habit, the owners kneed the dog in the chest whenever she mounted their legs. They also stepped on her feet, squirted her with water, or smacked her firmly with a newspaper.

The dog really could not help herself but the harsh measures got the message across and she became afraid. Then Ruth started mounting other dogs when her owners took her to the park. That is when they brought her in to see me.

"We cannot believe this bad behavior," they told me. But that was not the problem. It was bad hormones. Once the hormone imbalances were corrected, the problem stopped. That was four years ago and she has been normal ever since.

Epilepsy

Iris's owner carried her into my office. The two-and-a-half-year-old Irish Terrier was on massive doses of phenobarbital, yet having a *grand mal* seizure. She was shaking, frothing at the mouth, and her eyes were rolled back. She looked like a dog coming out of anesthesia.

The owner was distraught. Iris was the children's favorite dog. He had done everything he could for her and he did not know what to do anymore. Iris had been having convulsions on a daily basis for the previous six months. Somebody had told him I might be able to help but it was going to be his last resort.

I did the endocrine-immune test, identified the imbalances, and started Iris on a therapeutic program. I also determined that Iris had a serious case of malabsorption and as a result was not effectively utilizing the medication. I also suspected there were major food intolerances triggering the seizures.

The combination of hormone replacement and a closely monitored hypoallergenic diet resolved the epilepsy. Slowly, Iris was weaned off the phenobarbital.

Occasionally she has experienced minor, *petit mal* seizures as a result of somebody feeding her an offending food. Iris does not tolerate beef, lamb, rice, wheat, and eggs. The family is extremely vigilant about this problem. When guests come over to eat, her owners keep the dog in a separate room to prevent accidental food intake. Iris has not experienced a major seizure since she started on the therapy four years ago.

In an epileptic pet, offending foods can directly trigger a seizure even if you correct the endocrine-immune defect. You need to correct the flawed mechanism with hormonal replacement and carefully monitor the food. With this approach, dogs can be weaned off anti-epileptic drugs or given smaller dosages.

On a comprehensive therapy program, the veterinarian and the pet owner need to watch how the animal reacts to the phenobarbital dosage. As absorption improves from the therapy, more medication reaches the bloodstream and goes to work. With increased absorption, the regular dosage now may cause grogginess. Working with your veterinarian, you may be able to reduce the dosage without endangering the dog. Often you will be able to eventually discontinue phenobarbital.

Vaccine Reactions

A veterinarian was vaccinating Penny, a three-month-old Italian Greyhound. Ten minutes after administering the shots the dog suddenly had difficulty breathing. The dog's blood pressure dropped, her heart rate soared, and she keeled over. The veterinarian revived her but the owners were afraid to vaccinate further. They came to me for a second opinion.

Testing revealed that Penny had common hormone-immune imbalances that likely caused her dramatic anaphylactic reaction. An antibody titer test showed that she had not developed immunity from her initial vaccinations. I placed the young dog on a remedial program and then carefully re-vaccinated her without a problem. Penny, now seven, has not had any vaccination complications since her hormones were corrected.

Like Penny, I find that all pets who experience vaccination complications have endocrine-immune imbalances. I have treated several hundred dogs over the years with previous acute reactions to vaccines, such as vomiting, diarrhea, a breakout of hives, or bronchial constriction within eight hours of shots. Tests showed they were all hormonally imbalanced.

Not all the owners of these animals agreed to the therapy program. For the ones who did agree, their animals had no subsequent vaccination problems.

Bacterial Infections

Greta was a Doberman puppy with severe pustules on her chin, ankles, and elbows. She would constantly chew, bite, and lick them. I saw her for the first time when she was three months old. Previous antibiotic treatments had helped only temporarily. The bacterial infections had returned, and frustrated, the owners considered euthanizing her.

Greta had endocrine-immune imbalances with suppressed immune cells that could not overcome the recurrent infections. The pustules were the external signs of her defective genes. I kept her on the appropriate antibiotics just to get her through the transition until the endocrine-immune therapy kicked in. It has been thirteen years since Greta first went on the program. She has been fine ever since.

Skin Fungus

Bob, a Springer Spaniel, had suffered from chronic skin fungus since the age of six months. He had open lesions with hair loss and a moth-eaten appearance. His owners had given him oral medication and twice-weekly fungal baths to control the infection but nothing much had helped. The condition might improve a bit and then return.

I saw Bob when he was three. It turned out that he did not have a pathogenic fungus. His problem was a resident fungus that most dogs have but can normally keep in check. The dog's hormonal-immune balance was disturbed and as a result he was unable to contain the fungus.

Bob is eleven now and has had no recurring fungal problems since starting the replacement program. Once a year his owners bring him in for retesting. He appears capable of living a healthy life span to sixteen or so. I suspect he would have died at five or maybe earlier if his condition had not been corrected.

Fleabite Allergies

Endocrine-immune imbalances open the door for allergic reactions that can manifest anywhere in the body. You may see vomiting, diarrhea, chronic scratching or coughing, or even blood in the urine. The clinical signs develop in different impact areas that are genetically predetermined.

In Darby's case, it was the skin. This suffering Golden Retriever had severe hair loss and was constantly scratching from a fleabite allergy. The owners were so desperate that they had the dog wearing a T-shirt dripping with pesticides when I first saw her. She was six at the time and had been miserable her whole life. Fleas pick up on hormonal, immune, and nutritional weaknesses. Pets like Darby with pronounced imbalances become flea magnets.

After two weeks on the endocrine-immune program, she was on her way to recovery. The T-shirt was discarded, and so were the flea baths and flea medication. Her immune cells could handle the flea antigen. She was maintained on the program for the rest of her life and died at fifteen.

Food Intolerance

Over the years I have advised many pet owners to find non-offending foods for their highly sensitive animals. Frequently these owners had experimented with numerous diets. Unless you correct the primary problem, hormonal-endocrine imbalances, there is often little that highly sensitive animals can eat. They will continue to experience vomiting, diarrhea, skin disorders, and/or bladder problems. And even when the imbalances are corrected, a pet owner must make an effort to avoid exposure to individually offensive foods that still pose a potential problem.

Diik II was a Brittany Spaniel who started developing sick skin as a puppy. I tested him, identified the imbalances, and initiated a hormone replacement program. The dog was basically healthy but as he got older, we began to see signs of food intolerance.

In his case, the impact area was the urinary tract. Diik II had developed bladder inflammation and the owner came in after seeing blood in the dog's urine. Urine cultures were negative, so it was not an infection. It was an immune reaction to a specific food.

The immune cells remember. Even if imbalances are corrected the cells react to a previously offending food and cause problems in highly sensitive animals. I do not understand the mechanism involved, but simply put, the immune system does not forget a trouble-making food.

Many people believe that if you avoid a particular allergenic food for a month or so, as is recommended in so-called elimination diets for people, you can subsequently tolerate the particular food. I do not find that this happens in pets. It appears that once a reactive food, always a reactive food. Moreover, reactions can be more severe when you try to re-introduce an offending food after an elimination diet. An affected dog or a cat may be able to eat a certain food for awhile but then boom! I have not figured out how to beat food intolerance sensitivity. No matter how effectively the hormones are corrected, the wrong food can still set off a reaction.

Diik II did fine on lamb and rice for three years, but then developed an intolerance. I changed the diet to a food plan based on the Innovative Veterinary Diets. (See Chapter Ten.) The dog thrived, never developed further problems, and lived to be seventeen. Over the years his owners were extremely careful about food.

It is worth repeating that food is the only thing that can seriously undermine endocrine-immune therapy and cause a setback. If you feed the wrong food, the program will not work. Period. However, that is not the case with animals who have inhalant allergies, such as to pollen, or skin-contact sensitivities to such substances as fertilizers and detergents. Once you correct the hormonal imbalances, those particular sensitivities are no longer problematic.

Malabsorption

Jesse, a two-year-old Border Collie, looked like she was just liberated from a concentration camp when I first saw her. She had a major case of malabsorption. The dog was essentially dying. She had lost more than half her body weight and was down to twenty-two pounds. Her coat was thin and patchy, she was passing a large amount of stool, had a noisy, upset stomach, could not get comfortable, and was extremely restless during the night.

I corrected Jesse's endocrine-immune imbalances and prescribed a hypoallergenic diet for her along with digestive enzymes. She lived to be eighteen years old.

Malabsorption and Enzyme Deficiency

This case involved a very thin, two-year-old Tibetan Terrier with a chronic allergic dermatitis. Ralph had trouble absorbing the oral hormone I prescribed to correct his imbalances. He also could not handle his diet. The fatty acids in his food tended to sludge, coating his gut, and interfering with absorption of nutrients and the medication.

The dog's problem was a trypsin deficiency. It was readily solved by a digestive enzyme supplement that aided the breakdown of fatty acids. Subsequently, Ralph could absorb food and medication. He regained weight and his skin problem cleared up. (See more on trypsin in Chapter Eleven.)

I routinely put my patients on an enzyme supplement. It cannot do any harm and usually does a lot of good for most pets, particularly if they have food sensitivities and chronic disease. They benefit enormously from enhanced absorption.

Chronic Kidney and Bladder Disease

A two-year-old Cocker Spaniel named Blain suffered from chronic kidney/bladder disease. He was urinating in the house and his owners found blood in his urine. He had been treated previously by three different veterinarians with multiple antibiotics to control an obvious urinary tract infection. The medication helped temporarily, but the condition kept returning.

Cases like this are common. The bladder burns, the kidneys do not work well. Often, endocrine-immune imbalances are involved as an underlying mechanism, causing inflammation and irritation of the urinary tract tissue. Correcting the imbalances may solve an otherwise recurring condition.

In this case, Blain's owner had found a copy of my pet allergy book at a garage sale and bought it for fifty cents. In the book I mention the connection between a cortisol deficiency and deregulated immune cells that could affect the urinary tract. It just so happened that the owner lived near my hospital and immediately made an appointment.

I checked out Blain, did the blood test, and found the imbalances. Correcting the problem was routine and Blain normalized within one week. No more excess urination and no more blood in the urine.

Chronic Liver Disease

Doris, a six-year-old Irish Setter, did not want to eat. She had a swollen abdomen and from time to time became jaundiced. A previous veterinarian suspected a tumor. Several times he prescribed steroid medication to reduce liver inflammation and noted that the dog improved. However, the veterinarian always prescribed the medication on a short-term basis due to his concern about side effects and overloading a weakened liver. When the cortisone was discontinued, the condition would return.

Doris was brought to my clinic for a second opinion. I did not find a tumor, but I did find an endocrine-immune disturbance that I corrected with a long-term program of low-dosage cortisone. In addition, I prescribed thyroid medication to enhance liver function and help the dog process the medication out of the system. Remember that the imbalance also involves elevated estrogen, which tends to interfere with thyroid activity. This slows down the metabolism, including liver function. Even if thyroid hormones appear normal, the presence of higher than normal estrogen strongly suggests the need for thyroid supplementation. With cortisone alone, and no simultaneous prescription for thyroid, a buildup of steroid can occur in the liver even though the treatment utilizes a low dosage. Imbalanced dogs usually require both cortisone and thyroid for success.

Doris improved quickly on the program and lived a normal, healthy life. She died at age fifteen.

Liver problems are common. I see them often in Dobermans. The animals will have elevated liver enzymes, a sign of congestion and toxic buildup. A practitioner frequently will do a biopsy and diagnose a chronic active hepatitis. Hepatitis may or may not be involved, but most of the time I find easily correctable endocrine-immune imbalances.

Obesity

Bruiser, an American Bulldog, was forty pounds overweight by age two. He weighed 130 pounds when I first saw him. His owners fed him kibble based on the mistaken belief that kibble has less calories than canned food. It is just the opposite. But the dry food was just a minor part of the problem. The hidden problem was a cortisol-estrogen disturbance of thyroid function. Out of frustration, the dog's owners had limited Bruiser to a half can of dry food per day, exercised him vigorously, and yet he kept gaining weight. Once I corrected the imbalances, the weight started to drop. Within about a year-and-a-half, he was down to a normal ninety pounds. Six years later, he continues to maintain a solid, healthy body.

Obese dogs are routinely tested for thyroid function. Outside of an outright hypothyroid condition, the tests usually come back normal and veterinarians are inclined to think that the weight problem does not relate to the thyroid. Indeed the problem really is not directly the thyroid. The problem often is the result of cortisol deficiency, the production of excess estrogen, and subsequent interference with thyroid hormone activity.

To effectively help an obese dog, a veterinarian needs to test for total estrogen as I do in my endocrine-immune blood panel. If estrogen is higher than normal, suspect a binding effect on thyroid. Check the heart rate, and if below the normal 95 to 120 beats per minute, there is thyroid blockage, even if standard blood tests yield normal thyroid results.

With the underlying imbalance even a low-calorie vegetarian diet will not do much good. You will still have an obese dog. The problem is hormonally based. Correct it and the obesity is often resolved. I have successfully treated several thousand obese dogs with this program.

Autoimmune Hemolytic Anemia

Aemon was an Airdale who became severely anemic as a result of an autoimmune condition in which the body attacks its own red blood cells. A veterinarian contacted me from Sydney, Australia, where the dog lived and asked me for advice on how to help save the dying animal. Aemon was three at the time, depressed, lethargic, with white gums, rapid heart rate, and lack of appetite. He had a very low red count.

I recommended intramuscular steroid injections immediately. In a critical situation like this, a veterinarian should not initiate therapy with oral medication. There may be an absorption problem and you cannot take a chance. I also recommended thyroid supplementation for Aemon.

The dog responded. His red count went swiftly up to 36, which is low/normal. As his health improved, Aemon was soon put on oral cortisone medication. Within a half year his red count reached 42, a good level.

One day I received a call from Australia that the dog had suddenly taken a downturn. The white cell count had increased and the red cells had decreased. The veterinarian rechecked the endocrine-immune factors, which reflected imbalances anew.

It was not possible for me to determine the precise cause, but a malabsorption problem had apparently developed. I suggested returning to the periodic injectable therapy, injecting Aemon with cortisone every several weeks. (I describe that procedure in Chapter Nine.) Aemon recovered nicely.

The point of this story is that some animals cannot make it on oral cortisone medication. When signs of sickness return, retest the endocrine-immune levels. And even when the animal is doing well, I recommend retesting on an annual basis. This gives a good picture of what is going on.

Rheumatoid Arthritis

I usually resolve this autoimmune condition by correcting the adrenal defect. Buddy, a one-year-old Yellow Labrador, was brought in with multiple swollen joints. He could barely walk. The owner told me the dog had been under the care of a veterinarian who wanted to use heavy-hitting immune suppressant drugs. Concerned about side effects, she came for a second opinion.

I explained the probable endocrine-immune involvement and said that such powerful medication would do the dog in. If Buddy's immune system was already dysfunctional, why suppress it further? My belief is to put order back into the system, not hinder it.

The combination of low-dosage cortisone and thyroid restored order to Buddy's immune system. Within two weeks, the swelling went down and stayed down. The dog is now eleven years old and has no signs of arthritis, calcified joints, or inflammation.

Three Vizsla Littermates with Cancer

Hemangiosarcomas arise in the endothelium, the lining of blood vessels and the spleen. These extremely malignant tumors are most common in middle-aged or older dogs. Often, there is little warning before serious signs of disease become present. Once diagnosed, death can occur within a few months or even faster.

All the cancer patients I have ever tested, whether they have disease of the bones, blood, or the gastrointestinal tract, all have endocrine-immune imbalances. In my opinion, cancer is an end effect of this unrecognized disease mechanism.

A Vizsla breeder contacted me concerned that three of her dogs, all out of the same breeding but sold to different people, had developed hemangiosarcomas of the spleen. The animals were three years old and each one had a swollen abdomen following a rupture of the spleen.

In each case, the spleen was surgically removed. On the recommendation of the breeder, the dogs were tested for endocrine-immune status by their veterinarians. I was asked to analyze the results. All the dogs had imbalances. All three were put on the hormone replacement program and have been doing well. That was four years ago. Usually, animals die within six months after the spleen is removed.

Hormone replacement therapy benefits many of my cancer patients, but the best strategy lies in its prevention before there has been physical damage. Do the test, correct deficiencies if they exist, and you may substantially reduce the risk of cancer or at least delay it until much later in life.

— THIRTEEN —

Cats in Balance

I have selected a variety of cases to illustrate the effectiveness of endocrine-immune therapy as a healing option for cats. About 90 percent of affected cats do quite well on cortisol replacement therapy alone. Cats with feline infectious peritonitis (FIP) or with hypothyroidism also need thyroid medication as well.

Aggression

"The cat's always been a little strange, but recently he has been chasing after us and biting," explained Billy's distraught owners during their first office visit. They told me their neutered, two-year-old Russian Blue male was retreating to dark closets and then springing out to attack family members.

Unfortunately, more and more lately I have been hearing variations on this story. Some clients have had to seek medical attention after being attacked. I find the problem often relates to hormonal imbalances that can severely disturb an animal's emotional stability. The more pronounced the imbalances the sooner aggressive behavior is seen. I have looked into the eyes of these animals and often seen that they are ready to kill.

People often want to euthanize these animals. As an alternative I suggest trying the endocrine-immune therapy. This usually solves the problem. Billy was a routine case and a real pussycat after he went on the program.

Separation Anxiety

Flossie was a six-month-old Himalayan, a prized animal companion of a woman who had saved diligently to buy the expensive kitten from a fashionable breeder. Although very affectionate and lovable, Flossie turned into a raging tiger, tearing up furniture and curtains when her owner left for work each day.

Another veterinarian declawed Flossie in an effort at damage control but the destruction did not stop nor did the measure curb the extreme anxiety. The cat's nubbins were bloody from continually trying to claw at things, and she continued to bite and chew furniture, towels, and other household items.

The owner brought the cat in for a consultation. I explained the possibility of an endocrine-immune imbalance and how it could affect behavior. I tested the cat, found high estrogen, and suggested a hormone replacement program. Flossie quickly shed her anxiety after starting on oral cortisone. Although her owner continued to work and leave her alone for hours each day, the cat was no longer destructive. Flossie has been on a maintenance program for ten years.

Two Cases of Unnatural Spraying

A black and white domestic shorthair named Agatha had been spayed at six months. Several months later the owner began to notice the cat marking a wall and various pieces of furniture. Puzzled by this behavior, the owner took Agatha to several veterinarians who alternately suggested bladder infection, kidney infection, and food sensitivities. None of their treatments helped.

The owner brought Agatha to my clinic. She had a cortisol problem causing an excess of estrogen and testosterone release. As a result, the spayed cat kept marking her territory, like a typical unneutered male. Once the imbalances were corrected the spraying stopped. I have used the endocrine-immune therapy to eliminate this problem many times.

The same approach also works for neutered males who continue spraying. For example, Blackjack, a domestic shorthair, had been fixed at six months but afterwards suddenly started to spray. In cases like this veterinarians sometimes find a hidden, retained testicle that was not removed. If found, it is removed, and the spraying stops. But Blackjack had no retained testicle. His testosterone stemmed from adrenal dysfunction originating with a cortisol deficiency.

Whether a female like Agatha or a male like Blackjack, the cortisol defect can promote spraying as a result of unsuspected testosterone production. I prescribed a program of low-dosage cortisone for Blackjack, which corrected the imbalances and he stopped spraying.

Epilepsy

Ralph, a very sweet three-year-old domestic shorthair had suffered from severe epilepsy half his life. Another veterinarian had put him on phenobarbital, the anticonvulsant medication, however the cat still experienced seizures a couple of times a week with each seizure lasting several minutes. Sometimes he would have a series of minor seizures—called cluster seizures—over a day or two. Occasionally the owners had to take him to the emergency clinic for Valium to stop the seizures.

They brought the cat to my clinic because the owners felt they were not getting anywhere with conventional treatment. "We cannot stand to see him suffering any more," they told me. "Either you can fix him or we're going to put him to sleep." They also said that the previous veterinarian had found that the phenobarbital level in the blood was low. That fact, along with lack of control, strongly suggested the presence of endocrine-immune imbalances.

Skewed hormones can impact the central nervous system, operating as an unsuspected trigger for common idiopathic epilepsy. The imbalances also can disrupt immune function in the intestinal tract and create inflammation and malabsorption. Ralph was simply not absorbing enough medication to prevent or minimize the seizures.

I tested Ralph and indeed he had the imbalances. I started him on the injectable combination of long- and short-acting cortisone. (See Chapter Nine.) I did not want to use oral cortisone because of the probable malabsorption. I asked the owners to carefully monitor the cat's response to continuing phenobarbital because as the therapy reduces the gut inflammation, absorption of the anticonvulsant medication could be expected to increase. The drug dosage prior to therapy was insufficient to control Ralph. With therapy, the same dosage of phenobarbital could become excessive and cause grogginess and unsteadiness.

As the absorption increased, I asked the owners to halve the dosage of the phenobarbital. Soon I was able to eliminate the epilepsy medication altogether and switch Ralph to oral cortisone. He has been on the program now for ten years.

Correction of endocrine-immune imbalances prevents seizures in about 85 percent of epilepsy cases that I treat. This eliminates the need for epileptic drugs.

Ralph had a couple of seizures over the years that were caused by eating forbidden foods to which he was sensitive. This is always a danger. Sensitive animals who are otherwise controlled with hormonal replacement therapy can have a seizure if they eat an offending food. (See Chapter Ten.) Fish is the no-no for Ralph. The first time it was tuna. The second time it was leftover salmon intended to be a treat. Ralph may have enjoyed the treat but he did not enjoy the consequences.

Vaccination Complications

Jezebel had been vaccinated routinely and without incident, first as a kitten and then annually for a couple of years at another animal hospital. However, when she was three, the vaccination provoked an acute anaphylactic reaction within fifteen minutes. The cat almost died.

Jezebel was referred to me. I identified endocrine-immune imbalances, corrected them with low-dosage cortisone, and was able to administer vaccinations without any further problem. I believe that as the cat had gotten older the effects of imbalances became more pronounced. I suspected interference with thyroid function, causing a slowdown in the processing of the vaccines. An unidentified and uncorrected endocrine-immune defect often promotes severe reactions to vaccinations.

Coral, an orange Tabby, had been vaccinated routinely by another veterinarian. One day the cat apparently came in contact with an infected feline and subsequently developed serious signs of upper respiratory illness. The infection progressed into ulcerations in her mouth. Her veterinarian administered a blood transfusion containing the relevant antibodies, a timely treatment that no doubt saved the cat's life.

When Coral later developed an upper respiratory infection, her owner referred the cat to me. I did an antibody titer test and found that Coral had not developed antibodies against the virus. Her problem related to a suppressed immune system unable to respond to vaccines. Early in life she got by on maternal antibodies, but with time they were no longer present. An endocrine-immune test showed Coral to have a typical pattern of imbalance. I initiated a low-dosage cortisone program. Two weeks later, I vaccinated her. After another two weeks, I retested her for antibody titers. She was now OK, and protected.

Feline Leukemia Virus (FeLV)

By the time I see affected animals, they are often dying and there is an acute emergency situation requiring intravenous treatment. I figure I have one shot: intravenous drips with cortisone. If I am lucky, and it is not too late, I can save the cat. Fortunately, the approach works in most cases, and I have been able to rehabilitate many seriously ill cats.

It is worth mentioning again that testing positive for the virus does not mean a cat will get the disease. Positive animals should have an endocrine-immune test. If they are normal—no defect is present—monitor them and recheck them every six months. If they have the imbalances, correct them, and they will not develop the viral illness. You can keep the virus at bay.

Ben was a seven-year-old neutered domestic longhair with leukemia. He was referred to me after three other veterinarians could not help him. He had pronounced weight loss, hair loss, sunken eyes, and was dehydrated. He was sick for four months and now looked as if he was at the end.

I did the blood test. His endocrine-immune counts were off. He undoubtedly had malabsorption. I started Ben on a week of intravenous solutions to stabilize him and then treated him as an outpatient with periodic IM injections. I wanted to bypass the gut with the medication until I could reduce the inflammation. Many of these animals have malabsorption. That is why I use an IV or an injectable in the beginning. That way I know I am getting the medication into the system.

After Ben improved I switched to oral medication. However, in his particular case, he did not do well on oral replacement. So I have kept him on a once-a-month injection that the owners administer themselves. After five months, Ben shed the virus and tested negative for leukemia. It has been four years now and he has remained quite healthy, but he needs to be maintained on the monthly injectable—his ticket to health.

I have found that some FeLV cats simply cannot absorb oral medication adequately. These cats will do well in the hospital on IVs and at home on the injectables but if you try to switch them over to oral medication, even at higher dosages, they suddenly start to slip. I cannot precisely explain why this happens. It could have something to do with a resistant defect of IgA antibodies in the intestinal lining still causing some inflammation and malabsorption. Or there could be a combination of factors involving food sensitivities and enzyme deficiencies.

Even when all these points are addressed a physiological block may be present that just cannot be overcome. Keep this in mind when considering hormone replacement therapy for FeLV and the other retroviruses. I find that about 80 percent of retroviral cats can be maintained nicely on oral therapy. The rest will require a monthly injectable. In Ben's case, I could not solve his absorption problem, so he needed the injectable. I have many recovered FeLV cats like him who were once nearly dead but who have lived on for many years on the injectable.

A Russian Blue named Mark was an example of a FeLV cat who lived for many years on simple oral medication. He was brought to my clinic almost dead at six months old. He was wasting away with chronic vomiting and diarrhea. I tested Mark and found that he had the imbalances. I initiated IV therapy and he quickly perked up. Once stabilized, I gave him an IM injection and sent him home. Subsequently, I switched him to oral replacement therapy. Mark is now sixteen and has been fine all these years on a regular program.

Feline Infectious Peritonitis (FIP)

A one-year-old neutered male named Sandy was brought in more dead than alive with an advanced case of wet form FIP. The signs were bad: anemia, tremendous weight loss, malabsorption, sunken eyes, an abdomen full of fluid with additional fluid in the chest. The situation clearly called for initial intravenous treatment to push Sandy back into life. For five days he received infusions with lactated ringers (sodium and potassium), B complex, soluble cortisone, and antibiotics.

In this, as in all FIP cases, there was also a need for twice-a-day thyroid medication. Cats with other conditions usually do not require thyroid supplementation except for the cases where testing clearly reveals a low thyroid function. Results tend to be normal. In FIP the results are typically normal as well. In fact, thyroid hormone values test normal in 95 percent of FIP cases. Nevertheless, experience has taught me that in order for the therapy to succeed I need to go ahead with thyroid replacement as I outline in Chapter Nine. I do not quite understand the mechanism. Perhaps there is an autoimmune factor involved. However, I do know how to help sick FIP animals recover. To do that I use thyroid. It is a must! The cat will die otherwise.

Oral administration (.10 milligram per 10 pounds of body weight twice a day) works fine for thyroid medication even if malabsorption exists. The thyroid hormone molecules are small enough to be readily absorbed. By contrast, cortisone molecules are larger and not easily absorbed in a situation of intestinal inflammation and malabsorption.

It usually takes some time for sick, depleted bodies to respond to the therapy. In the interim, secondary illnesses must be treated and each patient is different. For instance, severe anemia requires transfusions. In the hospital, Sandy received 55 ccs of whole blood because his bone marrow and red blood cell production had been suppressed for so long.

On the seventh day I gave Sandy a long-acting cortisone injection. He was eating, looking brighter, and the red blood cell count was climbing. I sent him home for three days. When he returned, I rechecked the red count. It was elevating in a normal direction. I rechecked the cat again in another week and he was doing great. Basically within a month, Sandy was well on the way to recovery. I gave him another injection at one month, and then two weeks later started him on oral cortisol replacement therapy. Sandy continued to do well, and for seven years he has enjoyed good health.

As I mentioned earlier I can rehabilitate about 70 percent of sick FIP cats. The others are just too far gone by the time I see them. Veterinarians assume that FIP cats with clinical signs of disease are not long for the world. As long as standard therapies are used I agree. However, the endocrine-immune program gives sick cats a great chance to rebound. In this context, I cannot emphasize enough the importance of keeping a cat on the program and not listening to the opinion of others with no experience of the endocrine-immune approach.

I will never forget one cat who had severe FIP. The cat recovered, shed the virus, and for eight years afterward led a totally healthy life on the hormone replacement program. One day the cat's owner mentioned the cortisone treatment to a friend who was a pharmacist. The pharmacist said continued cortisone therapy was harmful and strongly recommended that her friend get a second opinion. The other veterinarian agreed with the pharmacist that cortisone treatment was not advisable. He said FIP cats cannot be saved, and recommended euthanasia. I was incredulous when I heard about it. They euthanized a totally healthy cat because the other veterinarian said it was not possible to do what I had done!

Feline Immunosuppressive Virus (FIV)

Dylis, a one-year-old gray and white domestic shorthair, was brought in to my clinic basically to be euthanized. She had been diagnosed with FIV and previously treated by three other veterinarians. She had severe weight loss, inflamed skin, extensive hair loss, and could not hold her food down. "If you're going to do the same thing as everybody else, let's put her to sleep," her owners said. "No," I answered. "I can try something different that has the potential to save her."

After examining Dylis I determined she was not that far along. She did not need immediate IV treatment as so many critical cats do. Instead, I chose an IM injectable combination of short-and-long-acting cortisone. The effect of the injection would last for three to four weeks. I did not risk using oral medication because I believed her intestinal tract was probably in turmoil from loss of mucosal tissue immunity.

Within a few days the owners reported that Dylis was improving. At the two-week mark I saw her again. She had already regained some weight. Her fur was returning and the skin clearing up. I rechecked certain levels to make sure that the cortisone dosage was appropriate. Then, at three weeks I re-injected Dylis and scheduled another appointment for three weeks later. When Dylis returned, she looked phenomenal. I then switched her to hydrocortisone, the natural cortisone preparation. Three months later she tested negative for FIV. Dylis has been on the program for more than five years and is doing great.

Upper Respiratory Virus

Upper respiratory disease is very common, and resembles asthma. The signs are chronic coughing, sneezing, and runny eyes. Cats often have a hard time getting rid of the virus. Christine, a six-year-old Red Point Siamese, had suffered with this illness for practically her entire life. An endocrine-immune blood test revealed a typical set of imbalances. Her target area was the mucous membranes of the respiratory tract.

I started Christine on oral cortisone medication and within two weeks she was healthy for the first time in years. The coughing, sneezing, and runny eyes had vanished. This is not an unusually dramatic recovery. I have seen many hundreds of upper respiratory cases in cats clear up quickly with this approach.

In some cases, the imbalances also affect the gut and cause malabsorption. Such situations require injectable medication. If a cat starts on oral therapy and no improvement occurs within two weeks, recheck the endocrine-immune levels with another blood test. A malabsorption problem exists if there has been no appreciable change in the values. At this point switch to an injectable cortisone. If the cat improves, but is not totally well after another two weeks, increase the dosage level. (Refer to my recommendations in Chapter Nine on what to do in cases of malabsorption.)

I usually have a 100 percent success rate against chronic upper respiratory viruses. The only question relates to whether the cat can absorb medication orally or needs intramuscular injections because of malabsorption. If a cat gets an injection and problems persist after several days, then consider food sensitivities. You must identify and eliminate offending food that is upsetting the cat and interfering with the therapy. Christine did fine on oral medication from the start and has continued to be healthy for the past seven years.

Feline Acne

A seven-year-old male Siamese named Anton was brought in with a typical display of blackhead pustules on his chin. He had had them most of his life. I checked his hormones, and they were off. I put him on oral cortisone and the problem cleared up.

About a year later, somebody convinced the owner that it was dangerous to keep the cat on cortisone indefinitely, so she stopped the medication. The acne returned and to such a degree that it caused a severe infection of the mandible bone.

The owner came back in a panic. "The cat has been healthy and problem-free, but he has a defect," I patiently explained. "The medication does not hurt him. The medication replaces what he does not have in his body. It enables him to stay healthy and not have acne." Anton has stayed healthy without acne for nine years now.

Fleabite Allergy

Malcom was a veritable flea magnet. None of the popular anti-flea preparations helped. As a consequence, this young orange Tabby scratched and dug his skin raw. He was like so many other cats with endocrine-immune imbalances that create a weakened animal who over-reacts to fleas.

I corrected Malcom with a straightforward program of low-dosage cortisone. Afterward, he was like Supercat. He repelled fleas and never again reacted to the fleas that did come aboard. Malcom is ten and has been basically flea-less for seven years. The hormonal replacement program usually turns a flea-infested cat around within a week or two.

Contact Dermatitis and Mold Inhalant Allergy

Melinda, a two-year-old spayed Abyssinian, was brought in with contact dermatitis on her underside. At different times of the year, particularly in winter, she would react to mold and fungi in the air by sneezing and coughing. Her skin would show pronounced inflammation. A simple cortisol replacement program quickly resolved her problem. Her skin cleared up and she stopped reacting to mold and fungi.

Whether the problem is carpeting, mold, or pollen, environmental sensitivities often improve rapidly with the therapy because the underlying mechanism that permits reaction is frequently the same.

Digestive Problems

Karen, a five-year-old Burmese, had been burping and vomiting her entire life. The cat's owner had suspected hairballs, diabetes, or chronic kidney disease. None of these problems had ever checked out. Hypoallergenic diets had not helped.

When I first saw Karen, she was severely underweight at three-and-a-half pounds. In good health she might weigh six pounds. The cat had hormonal imbalances causing an IgA deficiency that disturbed the intestinal tract and normal digestion. Once I corrected the problem with cortisone therapy, the immune system normalized. Karen was able to eat everything. She gradually gained her weight and health back.

Unsuspected endocrine-immune imbalances often lead to digestive irregularities. Cats usually respond quickly to the therapy. Accompanying skin problems clear up as well.

Inflammatory Bowel Disease

Cats with this condition usually become increasingly weaker from lack of nutrient absorption. They are often euthanized. Beverly, a Chocolate Point Siamese, had been healthy for the first six years of life. She was once a vigorous twelve-pounder. Then, within a year she lost four pounds and developed increasing signs of ill health. A veterinarian diagnosed inflammatory bowel disease and prescribed oral cortisone, but the medication was not absorbed. When the condition did not improve, the cat's owners brought the animal to my clinic. I tested her and found deranged hormones and immune cells. I suspected there was a good deal of swelling and malabsorption.

In cases like this I first normalize the gut by using an IM cortisone injection. This usually brings down the estrogen level and starts restoring coherence to the immune system, including the IgA antibodies that protect the intestinal lining. I typically treat these cases with injectables for about two months. I consider IgA levels below 60 mg/dl as an indicator of diminished absorption. The lower the level, the poorer the absorption. I have seen baseline values as low as 8. That means practically no absorption at all. Once the IgA level rises to 60 or above I switch to oral cortisone therapy. In my experience, that is the absorption threshold. After switching, recheck the levels in two weeks to ensure the absorption and utilization of the oral medication. If the estrogen level has increased, and IgA has dipped again, step up the dosage of cortisone as I describe in Chapter Nine.

Beverly quickly improved after the initial injection and has had no problems since. She is thirteen now and has been maintained on oral replacement therapy for years. This approach can help animals nearly all of the time.

Feline Urinary Syndrome (FUS)

Ricardo suffered from urinary tract obstruction. He had three previous acute episodes and was in the midst of another crisis when he was brought into my clinic. The owners told me that if nothing worked this time they wanted to euthanize their eighteen-month-old domestic shorthair. "But do not do anything invasive," they said. Previous treatments had included antibiotics, diet change, IV fluids, and passing a catheter up his urethra to flush out obstructing grit. Nothing had worked.

I put Ricardo on an IV drip with soluble cortisone, antibiotics, and B complex vitamins. The vitamins help profuse the kidneys and serve as a diuretic. I also applied a catheter to facilitate elimination of urine. I kept Ricardo on an IV for two days until his urine showed no more signs of blood. Then I removed the catheter but kept him in the hospital for another day to make sure he could in fact urinate.

I sent him home with an oral cortisone prescription, an antibiotic, and a hypoallergenic diet. Two weeks later, I rechecked the blood levels. I found his estrogen still a bit high, so I increased the cortisone dosage. When I checked the levels again they were fine. Ricardo has stayed problem free for seven years on this program. He never blocked again. Like him, most cats do very well on this therapy.

It is interesting to note that if FUS males undergo the surgery to open up the urethra, they no longer become obstructed. However, they still produce stones, still have blood in the urine, and still have bladder inflammation because they still have the underlying hormonal-immune dysfunction that allows the disease to happen in the first place.

Females also develop bladder problems, they just do not obstruct because they have a wider urethra. But females may be treated repeatedly for bladder infections that may be caused by similar hormonal imbalances. Be sure to see a veterinarian immediately if your cat shows any evidence of difficult urination. That includes frequent urination, blood in the urine, straining to urinate, and shaking his tail in the box as he attempts to urinate. With males, if there is blockage, you will also hear the cat yowling and see him licking his genitals.

Chronic Kidney Disease

The same IgA antibodies operating in the bladder are also present in the kidney. When they become destabilized because of hormonal imbalances the kidney tissue may degenerate at an early age. I believe that is why veterinarians are seeing felines die at age seven or eight from renal failure.

A classic case involved William brought to my clinic at the age of seven. He was a neutered, tiger-striped domestic shorthair, his teenage owner's darling. William was dying. He had been diagnosed with renal failure and was now in an acute crisis. Another veterinarian had given up on him.

I started William on IV fluids with antibiotics and soluble cortisone. This perked him up some. I did the standard tests. The kidney enzymes and the BUN/creatine level were elevated. BUN is an abbreviation for blood urea nitrogen. Functioning kidneys readily excrete nitrogenous residue, the waste products of protein metabolism. When the kidneys are ailing, the BUN level rises. Infection or inflammation of the kidneys can also elevate a renal enzyme called creatine. That, too, is a sign of damage.

As the nitrogen level goes up in a chronic condition a cat will drink a tremendous amount of water and urinate a good deal as well. There may be nausea and weight loss. The high nitrogen can also cause anemia and inflame the pancreas.

The endocrine-immune test showed that William was out of balance. After resolving his immediate crisis I sent him home with an oral cortisone prescription and a short-term antibiotic. His BUN/creatine level started to drop within two days and soon became normal. William lived to be sixteen years old.

I made sure William had a diet with "clean" food. Often veterinarians prescribe low-protein special diets for kidney conditions. More important than low protein is pure protein, so that the kidneys do not have an overload of unused, poor-quality protein to excrete. In my opinion, a "clean" diet for kidney patients means fresh, cooked meats like chicken, beef, lamb, rabbit, and venison—whatever the animal can tolerate. But the key is fresh meat. It can be organic but not necessarily. It just needs to be fresh. I avoid the standard prescription diets. For convenience, I often recommend the "Innovative Veterinary Diet" products that are available through veterinarians.

In many cases of chronic kidney disease, veterinarians may perform a renal biopsy in an attempt to determine what is happening to the tissue. They will often find inflammatory cells and refer to the condition as glomerular nephritis. Hormonal imbalances and dysfunctional immune cells underlie the problem. The kidneys cannot protect themselves. The filtration membranes thicken and are eventually replaced by fibrous tissue. As the condition progresses, the kidneys become progressively nonfunctional. Correcting the endocrine-immune imbalances always works if there is enough functional kidney tissue left to carry out the needs of the patient, and there are no secondary stones. X-rays are often indicated to make sure that there are no stones or tumors present.

Mammary Carcinoma

Friday was a beautiful gray domestic shorthair. At age six she developed a large mammary carcinoma, an aggressive cancer. Another veterinarian surgically removed the tumor but did not hold out much hope because of presumed metastasis. He suggested follow-up chemotherapy but doubted it would make a big difference. He gave Friday a few weeks to live.

Friday's owner did not know what to do and came to me for a second opinion. I examined the cat and did an endocrine-immune test. Friday was eating and looked well, so I did not believe that an IV drip or intramuscular (IM) injections were necessary. The results came back from the test showing deficiency in cortisol, high estrogen, and abnormal immune cells, a pattern I see with all cancers.

I first tried oral cortisone medication and rechecked the levels in a week. The levels had not changed. It was apparent the cat was not absorbing the oral medication. I then gave her an IM injection of the short- and long-acting cortisone combination. I rechecked the levels a week later and saw they were now moving towards normal. Two weeks later I checked again and the levels were normal. Friday, now seventeen, has been maintained all these years on monthly cortisone injections. The therapy was able to stretch a few weeks of expected survival time into more than ten years so far. The owner still cannot believe it.

This simple therapy can definitely produce what some people might describe as a "miraculous recovery." It can indeed extend the lives of cancer patients if their physical condition has not been severely compromised by the disease. I have had many advanced cases respond in amazing fashion. In general, though, the earlier in the disease process the greater the potential for containment and recovery. This program will often prevent cancer from recurring or spreading. It does this by bringing order back into a weakened, chaotic immune system.

The program offers a powerful alternative to limited options of chemotherapy, radiation, and surgery, although in many cases those types of treatments are clearly needed. When they are needed, endocrine-immune therapy is highly supportive. The other techniques target the cancer directly. The endocrine-immune program addresses the cause of the cancer—the imbalances that leave an animal vulnerable to disease.

I do not recommend chemotherapy for cats other than for lymphoma, a deadly, fast-growing malignancy that attacks the lymphatic system. Studies show that chemo, the most widely used form of treatment for this cancer, may keep a cat with lymphoma alive for four to six months. In my experience, chemo combined with long-term cortisone therapy usually works very well and contributes to a much greater survival time. I start affected animals on both therapies simultaneously. Some of these lymphoma cats have gone on to live ten years or more.

— FOURTEEN —

Prevention

Your pet may look healthy but is he or she carrying a ticking adrenal timebomb that can detonate sooner or later and unleash chronic health problems?

You can find out by taking your animal companion to your veterinarian and request the test I describe in Chapter Eight. This endocrine-immune analysis provides a precise way to identify the presence of imbalances and then gauge the effect of therapy if you choose to follow the program.

For a puppy or kitten you are considering you can ask for a modified version of the test (the E-I 3 test) when an animal is least six to eight weeks of age. The test measures cortisol, the thyroid hormones T3 and T4, and estrogen. (Refer to the reference ranges detailed in Chapter Eight.) Abnormal levels indicate likely health problems and veterinary bills in the future, and you may want to pass on that particular puppy or kitten. Hormone replacement therapy for a lifetime is the only way to effectively prevent problems for such an animal.

Testing aside, you can also look for visual clues that indicate an endocrine-immune problem. I highly recommend checking your pet to see if these clues exist.

Clue # 1: The Red Gum Line

This indicator is present in about 70 percent of affected cats and 20 percent of affected dogs.

Pull back your pet's lips so you can see the gums. Look for a bright red thin line just at the gum line that follows the curve of the teeth. The gingival flare, as I call it, is most commonly seen along the whole gum line, right and left sides, and top and bottom. Sometimes it is more prominent over the canine teeth because of their larger size.

The line indicates inflammation, and a clear signal of hormonal imbalance and IgA deficiency. IgA is the major antibody active in the mucous membranes and plays a paramount role in protecting the system from outside pathogens.

I have pointed out this phenomenon to many veterinarians who have inquired about my method. Most have not been aware of the red flare along the gum line. Those who observe it often relate it to a local disease of the gums but do not make the association to a general immune system disorder. The flare should not be regarded as an indicator for tooth extraction. I have successfully treated many animals with the endocrine-immune therapy for whom full extraction had previously been recommended by a another veterinarian.

In one interesting case involving a cat, a veterinarian had decided against extraction only because he found the same red marking back in the angles of the jaw beyond the teeth. He knew that the disease would still remain after he pulled the teeth. Instead of extraction, the practitioner recommended euthanasia. The cat's owner consulted me for a second opinion. I saw the red lines in the mouth. The cat also had had other health problems for several years. I treated the underlying condition, a hormonal imbalance. The cat has been normal for more than two years with an ongoing hormonal replacement program.

Along with the flare line, there may or may not be other chronic mouth problems. In the case of classical periodontal disease, the gums can be curetted and the patient given an antibiotic to counteract the involved bacterial infection. However, if the red line remains after such treatment, you are likely dealing with endocrine-immune imbalances.

Clue # 2: Gray Underside

This sign is seen predominantly in dogs and seldom in cats. Look at the pet's underside. Excess pigmentation, meaning the skin appears gray, dark, or black, indicates a likely estrogen-thyroid imbalance.

I have seen numerous Golden Lab puppies with black abdomens. For this I recommend the endocrine-immune test. If done, the results always come back with abnormal values. If owners do not want to do the test because there are no clinical signs of illness, I advise watching for allergies that often develop in dogs with the dark underside.

I observe this in dogs of all breeds. Some breeders have told me that all their puppies have the dark underside but insist there is no significance. I tell them that such pigmentation predicts problems sooner or later. It is not normal and generally means imbalances.

Clue # 3: Hot Spots

This is a sign that applies to both dogs and cats. Hot spots are raw wounds that have been licked, chewed, or scratched open. If this happens on a regular basis you are probably dealing with an allergic reaction, an expression of underlying endocrine-immune irregularities.

Clue # 4: Hyper Pups

If you are considering acquiring a small puppy, the following simple test can help you determine the behavioral status of the potential pet. Hold the puppy in your cupped hands on his or her back with the feet up in the air. If the puppy struggles excessively and frantically in this insecure position, the dog likely has an estrogen imbalance and will develop hyperactivity and perhaps other behavioral problems as he or she grows up. This test has worked as an effective indicator in about 90 percent of cases. A puppy without imbalances will tend to lie calmly on his or her back.

General Tips for Optimum Health

Creating the best possible health for a pet and preventing disease means upgrading your attention and care. In addition to identifying and correcting endocrine-immune imbalances there are obviously many other steps you can take on behalf of your pet. Here is a short list of considerations:

- First and foremost, see your veterinarian right away if you notice a change in your pet's health. Nobody knows your animal as intimately as you do. Do not wait for a problem to get worse.
- Feed the highest quality of food you can comfortably afford. Pet food has its share of junk food. And junk food—as with humans— creates junk health. Cooking for pets is obviously the royal treatment but may not be practical for busy people. If you feed commercial formulations, be sure to read the ingredient list on the

label. Avoid byproducts, chemical additives, high protein formulas, and munchies loaded with sugar, salt, coloring agents, and preservatives. Check out the healthier products in your favorite pet shop or health food store.

But no matter what you serve, always be alert to the possibility of food intolerance. A commercial diet containing many ingredients may increase the risk of sensitivity to one or more of them. Even the most wholesome of foods can be offensive, and cause reactions for some pets. See Chapter Ten for details on feeding a hypoallergenic diet and how to test for food intolerances.

- I recommend vitamin and mineral supplements, and digestive enzymes to my clients. If you can afford these nutritional extras, your pet will benefit. (See Chapter Eleven on how to use supplements.) Keep in mind that sensitive pets can react to offending ingredients in supplements just as they can to offending foods.
- Do not forget exercise. We know the importance of physical activity for us. It is the same for dogs and cats. Ask your veterinarian for suggestions about how best to keep your animal in shape.
- Keep your pet clean and well groomed. Whether you routinely bathe and comb an animal yourself or have the job done by a grooming service, the close-up inspection involved offers opportunities to spot trouble before it becomes serious. Early detection of a problem can make a difference.

The Ten-Point Hands-On Health Check

Some years ago I developed a ten-point health check for groomers. You can also apply this inspection guide if you handle your pet's bathing and cleaning.

1) General Impression

- Take a general head-to-toe look. Is the animal limping, sluggish, hyperactive?
- What is the pet's general attitude? This is important because it can reflect how the animal is feeling.
- Does the animal look too thin or too fat? Either extreme may mean a problem.

2) On the Grooming Stand

- Stroke and caress your animal, making him or her comfortable. Run your hand easily over the whole body. Caress the head, the shoulders, the underside, and backside. Look for any bumps, lumps, warts, cysts, or something out of the ordinary. This will also help you avoid combing or cutting into anything that might cause pain.
- When you run your hand over the animal's body, does it feel thinner than last time? Weight loss is a common sign of disease. Enlarged female mammary glands can be a tip-off to pregnancy or a false pregnancy.

3) Check the Coat

- Stand back and view the entire coat. How is the coat for an animal of this breed? Is it lustrous? How is the texture? Is it fine? Is it coarse?
- Are there any areas of hair loss? This can often be a surface sign of an internal disorder.
- What is the color? Are there any rust-colored stains? These could be signs of some disturbance, perhaps an allergy, where the animal aggressively licks or chews at his or her skin.

4) Check the Mouth

- First, check outside the mouth, look for any dermatitis, hair loss, or abrasions near the lips.
- Check the teeth. See if any are broken or coated with excess tartar. Fractured teeth are an invitation to bacteria and abscesses.
- Check the gums. Look for the red line or any signs of inflammation. Pale gums may suggest the presence of anemia. In cats that could indicate anemia, a common accompaniment of feline leukemia and other viral conditions. In an older cat, pale gums can indicate chronic kidney disease. If you see this, do not delay seeing a veterinarian.
- Look for any tumors or masses.
- Check the insides of the lips and under the tongue.
- Smell your pet's breath. If it smells bad, this is a sign of gum disease or digestive problems.

5) Check the Ears

- Lift the ear flaps, and look inside. Do you see any discharge? Is there a fetid smell inside the ears? A bad smell may signal an infection, excess production of earwax, an allergy, or the presence of ear mites.
- Is the earflap thickened? Reddish, thickened tissue may mean there is an allergic reaction occurring, and perhaps an infection. A reddish-blackish wax suggests ear mites. See your veterinarian.

6) Check the Eyes

- Look for clarity. Examine the iris, the round, pigmented membrane surrounding the pupil of the eye. Is there a film-like opacity covering the area?
- Look at the white of the eyes. Is there any redness? This is a sign of possible inflammation and infection.
- Look at the eyelids. Check for small growths, inflammation, or styes that may be bothering the animal.
- Is there excess spillage of tears, leaving a rust-colored stain below the eyes? This can suggest an allergic problem.

7) Check the Nose

- Is there any discharge from the nostrils? This could indicate a possible allergy or infection.
- Look for a loss of pigment on the nose. A black nose that turns lighter could signify a genetic defect or a mineral deficiency, or merely indicate excessive rubbing of the nose against the surface of a plastic feeding bowl while eating.
- Constant sneezing with blood in the discharge could signal the presence of a foreign body, such as a foxtail, piece of grass, or even a tumor.

8) Check the Rear End

- When emptying the anal glands, check the color of the secretion. Brown is normal. A yellow or green color may indicate infection or inflammation.
- Check the rectum area and tail for any growths. A bulge on either side of the rectum may be a perineal hernia.
- Check for signs of tapeworms: small, rice-like grains or balls around the rectum hairs. An affected animal will eat excessively to

make up for what the worms are eating. The coat will be coarse, and a potbelly is often present.

- Check the genitalia for irregularities and inflammation. Observe the testicles to make sure there are no tumors developing, and to see that both testicles are there. Some dogs are born with only one normally hanging testicle. The other is retained in the body. Studies have shown that tumors develop in 40 percent of undescended testicles.

9) Check the Paws

- Inspect the base of the nails for fungus or inflammation. Check between the toes for foreign bodies, such as foxtails or cysts that may be causing pain.
- Look at the bottom of the pads for any cuts or punctures. Redness and inflammation on the bottom between the toes can be a sign of an infection, fungus, or a contact or food sensitivity. Any raw skin on the feet or up the sides of the legs could indicate excessive licking or chewing due to an allergic reaction.
- Signs of licking on the top of the paws—a rust-colored stain but normal, non-inflamed skin—may mean poor circulation. Decreased blood flow can cause tingling paws that an animal will repeatedly lick. A visit to a veterinarian is definitely in order to diagnose a possible cardiovascular condition.

10) Check the Skin (after bathing)

- With a wet animal, you can get a good close look at the condition of the skin. Look for red, raw, or raised areas, signs of a current inflammation due perhaps to allergy or infection. Patches of thickened or black skin can be signs of past problems.
- Check for dark skin on the underside, which signals the presence of the endocrine-immune defect.

— FIFTEEN —

Breeder Responsibility

A smaller, more muscular shape; a certain tail length; specific hair colors and markings: these are but a few of the countless breed standards that govern the world of dog and cat breeding. Animals are mated for the purpose of achieving specific cosmetic results. Years ago, a cat breeder told me, "They're creating some gorgeous animals, but in the process creating a lot of monsters and animals who have no health and no longevity." Indeed, the actions of breeders have given new—and literal—meaning to the term "killer looks."

At great expense to the health of animals, breeding practices have taken a cosmetic/marketing path away from natural or functional criteria. As an example, this trend has converted hunting breeds of dogs into fashionable, nonhunting, household pets who have lost their field ability, nose, and hardiness. Pets have become more and more processed, unnatural, and unhealthy, and more like merchandise.

I am truly convinced that if current trends continue—emphasizing the latest fashion and ignoring the health of breeding stock—cats and dogs may simply be bred out of popularity. Whether they know it or not, breeders who worship at the altar of fashion and who relegate or ignore the health factor are compromising the survival of their breeds. They are, in a sense, practicing animal abuse. Their actions perpetuate unwellness and suffering. Their actions victimize buyers—innocent consumers who purchase puppies and kittens and who usually have no clue as to what may lie ahead in terms of sickness and veterinary bills.

I do not enjoy the sight of sobbing children carrying severely sick puppies and kittens into my clinic. I have seen too much of that: too many incurable animals bred for a miserable early death. Contemporary breeding practices carry the seeds of genetic disaster for animals and, ultimately, financial disaster for breeders. In time, people will stop buying damaged animals. They will be discouraged by escalating medical bills and witnessing beloved pets suffer and die prematurely.

We in the veterinary profession try as best as we can to rescue these animals from a quicksand of disease, from their own defective bodies that relentlessly suck them down. Based on my clinical experience, and conversations with many veterinarians around the world, conditions that could be easily corrected years ago are increasingly difficult to treat and more terminal. Many affected animals are so inbred that there is nothing anyone can do to help them survive. This situation is totally unacceptable and inexcusable.

Breeder Indifference

Irresponsible breeders are not interested in what I have to say. Responsible breeders are interested. "What can I do to correct this?" they ask.

One Standard Poodle breeder recently told me in tears that she previously had a six-puppy litter, all of whom developed epilepsy. And now she has three puppies with cancer. "What have I done?" she asked. "And what can I do?"

Testing showed that all the animals had imbalances. This woman has been breeding animals for twenty-five years and seriously considered quitting. "There is no need for that," I said, "there is just a need to correct what you're doing." And that is what we are working on together. This is a responsible breeder who cares and is willing to acknowledge a problem and take a remedial course of action. Her gene pool had just gotten too close.

Years ago, Roz Wheelock, a Doberman breeder in Riverside, California, started applying my testing and treatment program. "I have been breeding for thirty years but breeding smart for only the last fifteen," she says. "I breed first for good health and temperament, and then for show. In a breed that is riddled with health problems, my dogs are healthier, sturdier, and still can go out and win. Most of my dogs just do not see their vets except for vaccines. Many Dobies die at seven, eight, or nine. My dogs live on average ten to twelve years. Some go on to fourteen or so."

Wheelock is a breeder who cares, and who has taken responsibility. As a result, she offers her clients healthier and longer-living animals from a breed beset with health problems. Unfortunately, too many breeders do not care. They keep perpetuating genetic flaws and diseases, denying they have problems, and continue making the situation worse.

A prominent dog breeder commented to me that "if someone produces a beautiful line of animals that develops respiratory or allergy problems, that person may just continue turning out the line because it attracts attention and sales, and just ignore the health problem. Looks are by far the number one consideration." Events, however, will make such people care. They will end up with dead animals and dead sales.

A veterinarian friend told me about one of his clients with a Miniature Schnauzer who was maintained for years on the hormonal therapy program. When the dog finally died, the client said she wanted another Schnauzer. My friend suggested that she not go to the same breeder because he had been treating a lot of problems among that particular breeder's animals. The client ignored his advice and picked out a new puppy from the breeder. She did, however, bring the puppy to him at eight weeks of age for the endocrine-immune test. Results showed the puppy was totally imbalanced. The woman took the puppy back and received another one. My friend tested the second animal. The results were similar. The woman returned that puppy as well. She then went to another Miniature Schnauzer breeder and picked another puppy. The animal was tested and was fine. That puppy she kept.

It incenses me that unethical breeders continue creating genetic cripples, sell them at top dollar, but are not held responsible for what they have created. I think the medical costs for trying to keep a genetically impaired animal alive should be forwarded to the breeders. When the time comes that they have to pay for what they have wrought they will definitely care about what they are doing.

Today, too many breeders do not want to know or just do not care. It is an out of sight, out of mind mentality. They have happy, wonderful puppies and kittens to sell. When I describe the potential damage of endocrine-immune imbalances to these people they just turn off or go to another vet and call me a "quack."

I recall the case of a Golden Retriever who started to attack the owner. Another dog from the same litter severely chewed the housekeeper's fingers. I called the breeder after treating the animals just to let her know there was a problem. She replied that there was no problem and that I did not know what I was talking about. Her dogs were just perfect, she said.

I have encountered a lot of cases like this where breeders simply refuse to acknowledge a problem and their responsibility to correct it. It is very troubling. The same situation exists with cats. Something has to change—and soon.

Establish a Breeding Health Standard

In my opinion, we need to create a health standard that supersedes the fashion standard. Animals should be bred only after they meet solid criteria for health and vigor. Perhaps the endocrine-immune test I describe in Chapter Nine, and the one for puppies and kittens in Chapter Fourteen, could serve as part of such a standard. The test determines the basic health of an animal, and could be utilized both as a preventive and therapeutic weapon against the current genetic disaster. It also offers an opportunity for the future—for producing viable animals who are healthy as well as good looking. The indicators in the test can supply vital information as to which animals should—and should not—be bred.

I am encouraged by the fact that increasing numbers of breeders use the test's normal values as "passing mark" criteria for future breeding of animals. As they breed hormonally healthier animals they find much less sickness and more vigor in the offspring. In turn, the offspring are tested by the breeders and the best animals kept for future breeding. Less healthy ones are neutered or spayed and sold as pets.

This then is a predictability test that can serve not only to guarantee healthier offspring but also act as a diagnostic tool to help keep parents healthy as well. The test—and the accompanying therapy—is by no means the whole answer to the chronic disease epidemic, but I believe it can help reverse a devastating trend.

If you are a breeder and interested in this approach, here is what you can do:

Step One Do the test with your own breeding stock. If animals are imbalanced work with your veterinarian to correct the defect as I outline in Chapters Nine and Ten. That will help protect the health of those animals.

The practices of inbreeding and linebreeding need to be significantly reformed. There is room for flexibility here, but certain animals should not be bred to each other if they have similar genetic flaws or disease impact areas.

Step Two Have the test performed on any animal coming to you for breeding with one of your breeding stock.

Step Three Recognize the problem and the challenge if you have two imbalanced animals you want to breed. You do not have to be a geneticist to figure this out.

Both parents can have imbalances, but the imbalances cannot be in the same area. As an example I corrected a champion Brittany with a significant cortisol defect, very high estrogen, low thyroid hormones, and immune dysfunction. This was Candy, one of the animals I mentioned in Chapter One. Keep in mind that even though I corrected her she still carried the genetic defect.

Her owners were interested in mating Candy to a particular male with desirable physical and functional characteristics. I tested the male and found that he had only minor endocrine-immune imbalances. His cortisol was slightly deficient and the estrogen just slightly high. His thyroid hormones were fine. The animals were mated. The puppies were normal. I received one of the puppies, an elegant and healthy female.

Ideally the breeding stock should be "clean," that is, hormonally balanced. But nowadays there are not many clean animals. Many breeders do not want to admit their dogs or cats have imbalances. It is hard to sell something that is defective, and so they are afraid to actually test the animals. But even with imbalances, you can breed. Avoid breeding one animal with another if both have significant abnormalities of the same hormones as determined by the endocrine-immune test.

The therapy does not correct the genetics. It corrects the effects of the genetics that cause disease. If you breed two animals with the same degree of genetic flaws, even if both are corrected, then the genetic imbalances are merely passed on with more severe consequences for the offspring.

– SIXTEEN –

Implications for Humans

The knowledge gained from my clinical experience has profoundly expanded my understanding of how to prevent and treat diseases. I have learned that the primary triggers of sickness are often not the viruses or bacteria, or an inherent failure or weakness within the immune system to deal with disease, but rather a loss of hormonal governance over the system.

As a result of my successes and those of other veterinarians using this same approach, I have long wondered if the endocrine-immune testing and therapy program offer similar promise for humans.

I recently learned that a medical doctor has been using low-dosage cortisone with human patients for decades: William Jefferies, M.D., a clinical professor emeritus of internal medicine at the University of Virginia School of Medicine. Over the years, Jefferies has reported in great detail on his safe and effective use of cortisone medication for a variety of human illnesses involving what he calls adrenocortical deficiency. However, his clinical work has been ignored by most physicians. In Jefferies' words, the reason relates to the "unique situation in which a normal hormone, one that is essential for life, has developed such a bad reputation that many physicians and patients are afraid to use it under any circumstances."

I have repeatedly encountered this same attitude within the veterinary community, and often with hostility. At pharmacologic dosages, cortisone indeed creates side effects. Practitioners fear this. They generally shudder at any suggestion of long-term cortisone, even at smaller physiologic dosages acting as a hormone replacement for deficient cortisol. In a 1994 article in the journal *Medical Hypotheses,* Jefferies commented that most physicians practicing today are under the impression that any dosage of cortisone can produce any of the serious side effects that occur only with administration of large, pharmacologic dosages.

Jefferies has written extensively about his findings, including the book *Safe Uses of Cortisol* (Charles C. Thomas Publisher, 1996). From the human medicine perspective, he believes that indefinite replacement with low, physiologic doses of cortisone benefits many, if not all patients with allergies, chronic fatigue, and autoimmune disorders such as rheumatoid arthritis, and that replacement should not be stopped upon initial remission.

My experience with animals clearly validates this understanding. If medication is stopped, signs of illness return. That is because this application acts as a hormone replacement for a deficient hormone. If you stop the replacement, you still have the deficiency—and all the medical problems it creates.

Jefferies with humans, and I with animals, have discovered over decades of clinical work that regular daily low dosages of cortisone on a long-term basis are safe and extremely effective. However, if you were to use pharmacologic dosage levels that way, problems would certainly arise.

Recently, I have learned that other medical researchers are beginning to report successful applications of low-dosage cortisone in rheumatoid arthritis and polymyalgia rheumatica, a systematic inflammatory disorder of the aged.

Similarities to Immune Defects in Humans

My extensive search of the medical literature has not turned up anything exactly comparable to the scope of health-destroying suppression/destabilization of the immune system I find in household pets created by deficient or bound cortisol and elevated estrogen.

Congenital adrenal hyperplasia (CAH) bears some similarities. This human condition is characterized by a deficiency of cortisol and an increase in the male hormones called androgens, produced in the inner zone of the adrenal cortex. This increase stems from a deficiency in the adrenal enzymes that make cortisol. Once considered a rare inherited disorder with severe manifestations, a mild form is common although frequently undiagnosed. Patients with the mild form are frequently unable to mount sufficient stress responses to trauma and infection. CAH is treated, in part, with low-dosage cortisone medications.

Is it possible that a similar enzyme disturbance could be present in household pets? I cannot answer with any certainty because I have not found it necessary to the outcome of my treatment method to investigate for such a deficiency. However, this would certainly be a worthwhile study for veterinary researchers.

There are at least two clear dissimilarities between endocrine-immune imbalanced animals and CAH human patients. CAH creates an abnormal enlargement of the adrenal glands and a frequent deficiency of aldosterone, another adrenal cortex hormone. I have found neither of these among pets. Autopsies that I conducted years ago revealed cortisol problems in adrenal glands that were enlarged, shrunken, and normal. Apparently a defect can result with or without a change in the size of the gland.

I have been intrigued by striking similarities to immune deficiency syndromes in humans and to common variable immunodeficiency (CVID) in particular. Just like the unsuspected problem I treat in animals, CVID is a prime example of a widely underdiagnosed "enabling" mechanism for a multiplicity of disorders such as chronic infections, autoimmune conditions, poor response to immunization, and an increased risk of cancer.

In CVID, IgA, IgG, and IgM levels are low, just as in animals, and often there are also problems with T cell function. As the following list demonstrates, there are many other similarities between CVID and the endocrine-immune imbalance in pets:

- In humans, CVID was originally thought to be rare. It is now regarded as common. In pets, the endocrine-immune disturbance is common, yet unsuspected and unrecognized to date by official veterinary medicine.
- An interaction of genetic and environmental factors is involved.
- Diagnosis is confirmed by a low level of serum antibodies, usually IgA, IgG, and IgM.
- Medical effects can develop at any age. Symptoms can be mild to severe.
- One striking clinical feature is the chronic or recurring nature of infections.

- Infections are most often caused by the same organisms that trigger comparable infections in immunocompetent hosts, however immunodeficient patients develop infections as well from opportunistic organisms, even organisms of relatively low virulence.
- Both human and animal patients can develop severe infections, or complications.
- Both commonly develop enlarged lymph nodes.
- Both may develop painful inflammation of one or more joints called polyarthritis.
- Both may develop malabsorption.
- Some human patients develop inflammatory bowel disease and gastro-intestinal complaints such as abdominal pain, bloating, nausea, vomiting, diarrhea, and weight loss. Many animals experience such problems, which I believe is related to an IgA deficiency creating food sensitivity and inflammatory bowel disease.
- IgA is the most abundant antibody and is especially important in mucosal immunity, an essential protective factor against infectious agents, allergens, and foreign proteins that enter the body via the mouth, nose, upper respiratory tracts, the intestines, and reproductive tract. IgA deficiency is the most frequent immunodeficiency in humans and if it develops selectively it is known to evolve into the broader CVID. IgA has been of particular interest to me as a major yardstick in my assessment of disease and recovery. In animals, I routinely find a low IgA blood level associated with malabsorption and inflammation in the intestinal tract as well as inflammatory conditions in the respiratory and urogenital tracts.
- Infectious giardia, campylobacter, salmonellae, shigella, and rotavirus can become chronic and lead to significant weight loss. Such organisms in immune-compromised animals can be catastrophic.
- A subgroup of up to 30 percent of human patients develop autoimmune conditions such as immune thrombocytopenic purpura, autoimmune hemolytic anemia, rheumatoid arthritis, lupus, autoimmune thyroiditis, or primary biliary cirrhosis. In animals I see these same conditions as well as pemphigus.
- Patients can develop endocrine disorders such as thyroid disease or diabetes. Most canine patients have a primary or secondary thyroid imbalance.
- Among human patients there is an increased risk of cancer, particularly cancer of the lymph system, skin, and GI tract. In animals, all

cancer patients with all types of cancer have underlying endocrine-immune imbalances.

- Immunizations usually produce very low or absent antibody levels.

Humans with CVID receive gammaglobulin treatments that usually bring some degree of improvement. Some patients may require long-term antibiotics, something I have not found necessary in animals once the endocrine-immune imbalance is corrected. It would be interesting to see if the low-dosage cortisone approach, along with thyroid medication, offers greater effectiveness and relief of symptoms for humans.

In humans, the precise trigger for such immune dysfunction is unknown. Researchers have not linked CVID or other so-called immunodeficiency mechanisms to hormones. I suggest that exploring this connection, and looking at cortisol activity, may generate major clues for diagnosis and treatment.

Can We Learn from the Animal Experience?

Can genetic and environmental factors promote adrenal and immune defects in humans as they do in pets?

In dogs and cats, contemporary breeding practices have led to a plethora of genetic defects. Through testing, I have found that many puppies and kittens already have a cortisol problem and resultant endocrine-immune imbalances. If not corrected, the imbalances trigger health problems early on. The more profound the imbalances the more severe are the problems that develop. Milder imbalances, in combination with environmental factors such as stress and toxicity, promote the manifestation of disease later in life. Most litter members appear to be affected if one, or both, parents have imbalances. In some cases of human CVID, more than one family member is found to be deficient in one or more antibody types. One family member may have CVID while another has selective IgA deficiency.

In humans, cortisol has gotten a bad reputation because it becomes elevated by stress and can have negative affects on the physiology. The immune system, fertility, bones, weight, memory, and insulin activity suffer. But prolonged stress eventually exhausts the ability of the body to produce cortisol, creating a dangerous deficiency state. Jefferies has linked deficits to chronic fatigue, allergies, and rheumatoid arthritis in humans.

With generations of animals, I have witnessed an escalating severity of conditions related to cortisol problems. One can speculate that a cortisol defect could be passed on to offspring if both parents are affected. In dogs and cats this appears to be a very widespread problem. Is there a parallel development among humans with allergies and malabsorption in one generation and autoimmune diseases and cancer in the next? If the imbalance becomes expressed in children, could perhaps the impact of deregulated IgA create widespread loss of critical immunity in mucous tissue throughout the body? The effect could possibly create any one or more of the following conditions: allergies, hayfever, asthma, food sensitivities, malabsorption, or digestive tract, bladder, kidney and lung problems.

Can a comprehensive endocrine-immune strategy help human cancer patients? Imbalances exist in each and every animal cancer case referred to me. Importantly, therapy outcomes are usually positive, even in advanced cases when combined with excision, chemotherapy, or radiation.

What about AIDS? In cats, the feline immunodeficiency virus (FIV) involves a retrovirus similar to HIV. Veterinarians euthanize symptomatic cats, yet I have a 70 percent recovery rate among such patients. These cats remain disease-free as long as they are maintained on low-dosage cortisone. Cats testing positive for the virus do not "break" with clinical signs once they go on—and stay on—the program. I suggest that when a human is exposed to the HIV virus, whether or not he or she develops symptoms of AIDS may depend on the strength of his or her endocrine-immune connections. If an imbalance is found through testing, correction with appropriate hormone replacement could be a significant strategy for both prevention and therapy.

Can this mechanism contribute to human inflammatory bowel conditions such as colitis and Crohn's disease? There is currently an epidemic of inflammatory gut conditions among dogs and cats and I consistently find the imbalance in affected animals. The therapy works well. The typical low cortisol/high estrogen combination destabilizes and depletes IgA, a global antibody most active in the mucous membranes of the body, including the gut lining. Low IgA suggests an absorption problem. The animal (or human) may not absorb oral medication.

Therefore, I begin therapy with intramuscular injections of cortisone, or, in the case of life-threatening conditions, intravenous drips, along with thyroid replacement and a hypoallergenic diet. This total approach quickly lowers the estrogen level and raises IgA. The less-stimulatory food, as an adjunct, minimizes the risk of food-related reactions. Once IgA rises to a certain point, the inflammation subsides and I switch to oral medication. The same approach works for IgA-related conditions elsewhere. Animals with chronic bowel disorders (including food allergies), respiratory and urinary tract disorders, and anaphylactic and vaccine reactions invariably have abnormal IgA levels.

I have talked to many physicians about my findings in animals because I strongly believe that they offer genuine insights into human illness. The work of Jefferies certainly is one indication that cortisol deficiencies can trigger major problems.

Testing for Endocrine-Immune Imbalances in Humans

Patients can be retested after biweekly or monthly intervals to monitor changing relationships. The bottom line is that hormonal replacement must be measured against B and T cell levels.

For female patients, clinicians would have to consider ovarian estrogen. The level of total estrogen will obviously vary according to monthly cycle, age, and use of birth control pill or estrogen replacement. Reproductive age females might be tested in mid-cycle when the ovarian estrogen level is highest and again just prior to menses when it is at the lowest level.

The estrogen issue is central, I believe. My clinical experience shows that cortisol and estrogen have pivotal influence on immune function. Specifically, insufficient cortisol creates elevated estrogen through disturbed hypothalamus-pituitary-adrenal feedback. The net effect is to destabilize and undermine immune function, creating a vulnerability to different disease processes.

One way to prove such an unrecognized estrogen involvement would be a trial with symptomatic postmenopausal women who are not on estrogen replacement therapy. A study should include a baseline blood test of cortisol, total estrogen, T3/T4, and antibody levels, particularly IgA, IgG, and IgM. Such testing may reveal a pattern of low cortisol, high estrogen, and low antibodies, similar to what is found in household pets with clinical signs of disease. The clinician might also want to obtain a twenty-four-hour urine sample from the patient in order to test for active hormones and any other relevant markers. This would allow a comparison to blood values, which may test out as normal but in fact involve significantly bound hormones. Often it is not known if the hormone is working or not. The urine test can help clear up this question and contribute to a more effective treatment.

High estrogen would be considered an unexpected finding in a biologically aged group where estrogen is typically deficient. However, research indicates that estrogen synthesis increases in non-ovarian tissues as a function of age. In acute illnesses of postmenopausal women, there is a marked increase in the ratio of estrogens to androgens. Such conditions include heart attack, unstable angina, respiratory illnesses, and congestive heart failure.

Estradiol, and not total estrogen, is the standard estrogen for measurement in patients. I believe that total estrogen is a more meaningful indicator and should be measured instead. Estrone is the major estrogen in postmenopausal women. The serum level of estradiol is often less than 20 pg/ml in postmenopausal women and that of estrone, 15-18 pg/ml (26). One physician with whom I have talked extensively about estrogen commented that his sickest (non-ERT) postmenopausal patients have the highest total estrogen levels and the lowest immunoglobulins. Indications suggest a correlation of elevated estrogen with disease in the postmenopausal female, even though little is known about the factors that regulate estrogen production in this age group.

If researchers conducted clinical trials for humans using low-dosage cortisone and this resulted in a reduction of the estrogen level and of symptoms, as occurs in pets, one might assume that a cortisol defect with wide systemic impact has been corrected. Such a result suggests the therapy transcends mere symptomatic relief and argues for consideration of proper testing and the application of carefully measured cortisone replacement therapy.

Chemicals that mimic estrogens (so-called xenoestrogens) could also be involved in estrogen imbalance. Such compounds appear in the environment and in food. Ubiquitous estrogenic compounds, including industrial chemicals, pesticides, and surfactants, have been found to affect the immune system in wildlife and laboratory animals. Further studies are needed to determine the immune response in humans, however there is suspicion that these compounds may affect humans in similar ways.

In 1999, University of California-San Francisco researchers showed for the first time that dietary phytoestrogen compounds found in soy decrease cortisol production and, as a result, increase androgens. Such consumption, by raising DHEA and DHEA-S levels could indirectly increase total estrogen, the researchers suggested, and added: "Thus, it is possible that some of the estrogenic actions of dietary phytoestrogens may be mediated via their stimulation of adrenal androgen synthesis."

One way to determine the influence of dietary phytoestrogens, at least in men and postmenopausal women, would be to eliminate such food from the diet in a patient who has tested high for total estrogen. Retest the patient again after several weeks. A clear drop in the estrogen level could indicate a dietary effect. An unchanged or insignificantly changed level would indicate another source for the estrogen, such as conversion from androgens.

Xenoestrogens also include birth control pills and chemicalized estrogen drugs. Can these contribute to a disturbance of cortisol and thyroid, and contribute to the disease process? It seems plausible that adding exogenous estrogen, or even androgen supplements (such as DHEA, which can convert to estrogen in the body) could lay the groundwork for disease.

However, the fact that male animals develop elevated estrogen levels makes a strong case for cortisol deficiency as the primary cause. In symptomatic males with the endocrine-immune imbalance, the high estrogen occurs almost exclusively as a result of a cortisol problem. The rare exception is the animal who normalizes without any treatment after moving to another area. The assumption is that a significant xenoestrogenic compound, perhaps ingested or inhaled, was present in one area and not in the other.

A Final Word

Over many years of veterinary practice it has been my great joy to facilitate the recovery of many seriously sick patients. This has been a sustaining source of fulfillment for me.

Doctors learn from their patients—whether the patients are animals or people. I have always hoped that the lessons I learned could in some way extend beyond the field of veterinary medicine and be of some benefit to human patients.

I make no pretense about understanding all the molecular small print involved in endocrine-immune imbalances. I was fortunate to uncover some major channels of disturbed hormone and immune relationships and find a straightforward way to repair them and put pets out of harm's way. I strongly believe this experience argues for serious research to explore the nature, magnitude, and impact of cortisol defects, including an associated estrogen-immune problem as a cause of disease. Such research is beyond the ability of a practitioner like myself. Testing for the imbalance and correcting the cortisol defect, if it exists, could perhaps help reduce chronic health disorders in children and adults. The approach could perhaps also increase the effectiveness of oral medication that may not be absorbed adequately because of a low IgA level, the result of hormonal imbalances.

I suspect that a mechanism of unrecognized hormonal-immune imbalance is at play in human pathology. Surely the evidence I have gathered from treating generations of animals, and the evidence gathered by Jefferies, his followers, and other researchers, makes a strong case for vigorously exploring this issue.

I have spoken about my clinical work to the physician members of the Broda O. Barnes M.D. Research Foundation in Trumbull, Connecticut. Barnes was the doctor who discovered that many individuals have low thyroid function, and suffer many common ailments as a result, despite normal blood tests. I am pleased to be in continuing communication with some of these physicians. I am hopeful that these contacts will produce important revelations that will benefit human patients.

One such doctor, David Brownstein, M.D., of West Bloomfield, Michigan, says that what I have found in animals appears to be true also in humans. "The same pattern of hormonal imbalances and immune dysfunction you see in animals is clearly evident in many of my very sick patients," he has told me. "The same things are there. The adrenal malfunction, the high estrogen, and immune system failure with inadequate B and T cells."

A major focus of Brownstein's practice is aimed at balancing hormones and enhancing immune system function. To help achieve these goals he often uses long-term physiologic dosages of cortisone, following the example of Jefferies.

"Even though we are criticized by other doctors for using cortisone in this way, those of us doing it are delighted with the results," Brownstein related. "This method safely produces major benefits to patients. The potential here is huge for carrying out safe and effective therapies for many hitherto untreatable conditions."

In the past, many of my clients have asked if there were any medical doctors doing the kind of treatments for humans that I was doing for animals. I was not aware of any. But the day is at hand that I can start providing referrals. (Check my website for future referrals: www.drplechner.com.)

My clinical experience with animals shows that hormonal imbalances devastate the immune system and lead to catastrophic illness. This unrecognized yet widespread endocrine-immune syndrome needs to be identified and controlled. Adrenal gland function is central to health and proper cortisol balance is a key to good health and longevity.

RESOURCES

ENDOCRINE-IMMUNE RESOURCES

To read more about Dr. Plechner's research, articles in medical journals, and updates on endocrine-immune testing and treatment, visit his Internet website at www.drplechner.com.

TESTING

As of summer 2003, the following laboratories offer the Plechner endocrine-immune tests to veterinarians:

National Veterinary Diagnostic Services
Phone: (877) VETS LAB (838-7522)
Website: www.national-vet.com

IDEXX Laboratory Services
Phone: (800) 444-4210
Website: www.idexx.com

Antech Diagnostics
Phone: (800) 872-1001 (East), (800) 745-4725 (West)
Website: www.antechdiagnostics.com

ENDOCRINE-IMMUNE THERAPY PROGRAM

As of summer 2003, the following veterinarians use the Plechner Endocrine-Immune Therapy Program in their clinics. Visit Dr. Plechner's website for updates: www.drplechner.com

Tina Aiken
Pine Plains Veterinary Associates
2826 Church St.
Pine Plains, NY 12567
Phone: (518) 398-9494

Dwight A. Benesh
Chandler Small Animal Clinic
1286 W. Chandler Blvd.
Chandler, AZ 85224
Phone: (480) 963-3003

Cindi Bossart
Animal Hospital of
Ft. Lauderdale
1630 E. Oakland Park Blvd.
Ft. Lauderdale, FL 33334
Phone: (954) 561-8777

Angela Erickson-Greco
Animal Health Practice
355 Salmon Brook St.
Granby, CT 06035
Phone: (860) 653-2257

Gerald M. Gardner
(Equine practice)
1545 El Monte Drive
Thousand Oaks, CA 91362
Phone: (805) 495-2449

Bill Greer
Calzona Mobile
Veterinary Clinic
RR 1, Box 17483 S. B½
Somerton, AZ 85350
Phone: (928) 627-3527

Tyson Grover
Danada Veterinary Hospital
1 Rice Lake Square
Wheaton, IL 60187
Phone: (630) 665-6161

Curt D. Heyde
Pets First Veterinary Center
924 Haverford Rd.
Bryn Mawr, PA 19010
Phone: (610) 525-5041

J. R. Holcomb III
Hill Country Animal Hospital
7023 Bee Cave Rd.
Austin, TX 78746
Phone: (512) 329-5177

David W. Knaak
Limestone Companion
Animal Hospital
4224 S. Airport Rd.
Bartonville, IL 61607
Phone: (309) 697-8000

William R. Kroll
Viscaya Prado Veterinary
Hospital
920 Country Club Blvd.
Cape Coral, FL 33990
Phone: (239) 574-6171

Jim Nyholt
Antelope Valley Animal Hospital
1326 West Ave. N
Palmdale, CA 93551
Phone: (661) 273-1234

Kurt D. Oliver
Veterinary Associates Stonefield
203 Moser Rd.
Louisville, KY 40223
Phone: (502) 245-7863

Brian Reeves
Reeves Veterinary Clinic
2101 SSE Loop 323
Tyler, TX 75701
Phone: (903) 595-1088

David M. Schwartz
Downtown Birmingham
Veterinary Clinic
280 Daines Suite 100A
Birmingham, MI 48009
Phone: (248) 642-6144

Jim Simpson
Berryhill Veterinary Hospital
19073 S. Beavercreek Rd.
Oregon City, OR 97045
Phone: (503) 650-1667

Smith Ridge Vet Center
230 Oakridge Commons Plaza
South Salem, NY 10590
Phone: (914) 533-6066

Christine Sontag
Animal Medical Center
322 N. Metro Drive
Appleton, WI 54913
Phone: (920) 749-1717

Glenn R. Thorson
Boston Hts Veterinary Hospital
7040 Walters Rd.
Hudson OH 44236
Phone: (330) 653-2002

REFERENCES ON ENDOCRINE-IMMUNE IMBALANCES

Plechner AJ, Zucker M. *Pet Allergies: Remedies for an Epidemic.* Inglewood, CA: Very Healthy Enterprises, 1986.

Plechner, AJ. Chaos in the Cortex: Adrenal-Immune Disturbance in Pets May Offer Insights for Immune Deficiency Disorders in Humans (letter). *Townsend Letter for Doctors and Patients,* June, 2003: 122-124.

Plechner, AJ. Chaos in the Cortex: An unrecognized adrenal-immune disturbance in pets offers therapeutic insights for multiple human disorders. *Townsend Letter for Doctors and Patients,* April, 2003: 58-61.

Plechner AJ. An effective veterinary model may offer therapeutic promise for human conditions: roles of cortisol and thyroid hormones. *Medical Hypotheses,* 2003, 60 (3): 309-314.

Plechner AJ. Preliminary observations on endocrine-associated immunodeficiencies in dogs—a clinician explores the relationship of immunodeficiencies to endocrinopathy. *Modern Veterinary Practice,* October 1979; 811.

Plechner AJ. Theory of endocrine-immune surveillance. *California Veterinarian,* January 1979; 12.

Plechner AJ, Shannon M, Epstein A, Goldstein E, Howard EB. Endocrine-immune surveillance. *Pulse,* June-July,1978.

Plechner AJ, Shannon M. Canine immune complex diseases. *Modern Veterinary Practice,* November 1976; 917.

CHAPTER TWO
Lemonick MD. A Terrible Beauty: An obsessive focus on show-ring looks is crippling, sometimes fatally, America's purebred dogs. *Time,* December 12, 1994; 65.

CHAPTER THREE
Nelson DH, Samuels LT. A method for the determination of 17-hydroxycorticosteroid in the blood. *Journal of Clinical Endocrinology,* 1952, 12: 519-26.

Roberts E. The importance of being dehydroepiandosterone sulfate (in the blood of primates): A longer and healthier life? *Biochemical Pharmacology,* 1999, 57: 329-346.

Symington Thomas. *Functional Pathology of the Human Adrenal Gland.* Edinburgh: E & S. Livingstone, Ltd., 1969.

CHAPTER FOUR
Finkelstein J, et al. Estrogen or testosterone increases self-reported aggressive behaviors in hypogonadal adolescents. *Journal of Clinical Endocrinology and Metabolism,* 1997, 82 (8): 2433-38.

CHAPTER SIX
Cone M. Bear Trouble. *Smithsonian,* April 2003, 68-74.

Harvey PW. *The Adrenal in Toxicology: Target Organ and Modulator of Toxicity.* London: Taylor & Francis, 1996.

Harvey PW, Johnson I. Approaches to the assessment of toxicity data with endpoints related to endocrine disruption. *Journal of Applied Toxicology,* 2002, 22: 241-247.

Centers for Disease Control and Prevention. Overview of Vaccine Safety. Hurwitz E. Parents should know both the benefits and risks of vaccinations. *Los Angeles Times,* January 30, 2001: B9.

Moss W, Lederman H. Immunization of the immunocompromised host. *Clinical Focus on Primary Immune Deficiencies,* October 1998, 1 (1): 2.

Smith CA. Are we vaccinating too much? *Journal of the American Veterinary Medical Association,* 1995, 207 (4): 421-425

CHAPTER EIGHT
Takahashi I, Kiyono H. Gut as the largest immunologic tissue. *Journal of Parenteral Enteral Nutrition,* 1999, 23: Supplement S7-12.

Primary immunodeficiency diseases. *Clinical and Experimental Immunology,* 1999, 118 (supplement 1): 17)

CHAPTER SIXTEEN
Jefferies, W. *Safe Uses of Cortisol.* Springfield: Charles C. Thomas, Publisher, Ltd., 1996.

Jefferies W. Mild adrenocortical deficiency, chronic allergies, autoimmune disorders and the chronic fatigue syndrome: A continuation of the cortisone story. *Medical Hypotheses,* 1994, 42: 183-189.

Hickling P, et al. Joint destruction after glucocorticoids are withdrawn in early rheumatoid arthritis. *British Journal of Rheumatology,* 1998; 37: 930-936.

Cutolo M, Seriolo B, Villaggio B, Pizzorni C, Craviotto C, Sulli A. Androgens and estrogens modulate the immune and inflammatory responses in rheumatoid arthritis. *Annals of the New York Academy of Sciences,* June 2002, 966: 131-42.

Cutolo M, et al. Cortisol, dehydroepiandrosterone sulfate, and androstenedione levels in patients with polymyalgia rheumatica during twelve months of glucocorticoid therapy. *Annals of the New York Academy of Sciences,* June 2002, 966: 91-96.

Deaton M, et al. Congenital adrenal hyperplasia: Not really a zebra. *American Family Physician,* March 1, 1999: 1190.

Towson MD. *Common Variable Immunodeficiency: Patient and Family Handbook for Primary Immune Deficiency Diseases.* Immune Deficiency Foundation. Third Edition, 2001.

Gruber CJ, Tschugguel W, Schneeberger C, Huber JC. Production and actions of estrogens. *New England Journal of Medicine,* 2002, 346 (5): 340-52.

Spratt DI, Longcope C, Cox PM, Bigos ST, Wilbur-Welling C. Differential changes in serum concentrations of androgens and estrogens (in relation with cortisol) in postmenopausal women with acute illness. *Journal of Clinical Endocrinology and Metabolism,* 1993, 76 (6): 1542-7.

Ahmed SA. The immune system as a potential target for environmental estrogens: a new emerging field. *Toxicology,* 2000, 7 (150): 191-206.

Mesiano S, Katz SL, Lee JY, Jaffe RB. Phytoestrogens alter adrenocortical function: genistein and daidzein suppress glucocorticoid and stimulate androgen production by cultured adrenal cortical cells. *Journal of Clinical Endocrinology and Metabolism,* 1999, 84 (7): 2443-8.

ABOUT THE AUTHORS

DR. PLECHNER
AND BRUISER

Alfred J. Plechner, D.V.M., a 1966 graduate of the University of California-Davis School of Veterinary Medicine, has practiced in West Los Angeles for more than thirty-five years. Early in his career he developed a special interest in nutrition, allergy, and the relationship of hormone-immune imbalances to disease in dogs, cats, and horses. His research and clinical findings have been published in veterinary and human medical journals as well as popular animal magazines. His first book, *Pet Allergies: Remedies for an Epidemic,* was co-authored with Martin Zucker in 1986.

Over the years, Dr. Plechner has formulated a number of widely distributed commercial diets for food-sensitive pets, including the first non-meat and lamb and rice recipes.

Dr. Plechner has worked for many years with the California Department of Fish and Game and the U.S. Wildlife Service to establish treatment and care guidelines for rescued wildlife. His federal and state-licensed facility in the Santa Monica Mountains near Los Angeles serves as a relocation/rehabilitation center for rescued and injured wildlife indigenous to Southern California.

MARTIN ZUCKER

MARTIN ZUCKER has written extensively on health and medicine for twenty-five years. A former foreign correspondent with Associated Press, he has written or co-written more than ten books. His most recent are *Preventing Arthritis* (G. P. Putnam's Sons, 2001) and *Natural Hormone Balance for Women,* (Pocket Books, 2001).

Martin Zucker has written five books on pet health, including *Pet Allergies* (Very Healthy Enterprises, 1986) with Alfred Plechner, *The Veterinarians' Guide to Natural Remedies for Dogs,* and *The Veterinarians' Guide to Natural Remedies for Cats* (Three Rivers Press/Crown, 2000).

INDEX

OTHER TITLES BY NewSage PRESS

NewSage Press has published several titles related to animals. We hope these books will inspire humanity towards a more compassionate and respectful treatment of all living beings.

Food Pets Die For: Shocking Facts About Pet Food
by Ann N. Martin

Protect Your Pet: More Shocking Facts
by Ann N. Martin

When Your Pet Outlives You:
Protecting Animal Companions After You Die
by David Congalton & Charlotte Alexander
Award Winner, CWA Muse Medallion 2002

Blessing the Bridge:
What Animals Teach Us About Death, Dying, and Beyond
by Rita M. Reynolds

Three Cats, Two Dogs, One Journey Through Multiple Pet Loss
by David Congalton
Award Winner, Merial Human-Animal Bond, Best Book

Conversations with Animals: Cherished Messages and Memories
as Told by an Animal Communicator
by Lydia Hiby with Bonnie Weintraub

Polar Dream: The First Solo Expedition by a Woman and
Her Dog to the Magnetic North Pole
by Helen Thayer, Foreword by Sir Edmund Hillary

The Wolf, the Woman, the Wilderness:
A True Story of Returning Home
by Teresa Tsimmu Martino

Singing to the Sound: Visions of Nature, Animals & Spirit
by Brenda Peterson

Unforgettable Mutts: Pure of Heart Not of Breed
by Karen Derrico

NewSage Press
PO Box 607, Troutdale, OR 97060-0607

Phone Toll Free 877-695-2211, Fax 503-695-5406
Email: info@newsagepress.com, or www.newsagepress.com

Distributed to bookstores by Publishers Group West
800-788-3123, PGW Canada 800-463-3981